When Things Seem Impossible

Jean Dye Johnson

Twelfth Printing 2006

WHEN THINGS SEEM IMPOSSIBLE
formerly GOD AT THE CONTROLS

1000 East First Street
Sanford, FL 32771-1487

Library of Congress Catalog Card Number: 86-61860

Printed in the United States of America

Foreword

The true story contained in this book is an intriguing encounter with the Enemy, one that will hold your attention for hours. Because it documents the powerful hand of God moving through one threatening scene after another, your faith will be strengthened. It stands as undisputed evidence that our God is great and greatly to be praised!

Of the four missionary hostages mentioned in these pages, I know only one personally. I am delighted that I have met such a man as Paul Dye. Faithful to the core, he has spent years in the country of Colombia as a rugged missionary pilot. With his wife Patricia and their three children, Paul has served the cause of Christ without one ounce of reservation. We need such people as the Dyes, the Cains and the Estelles to look up to, and so do our teens and children. God has always used certain men and women to shape others' lives. Those who stand in the gap, however, are few in number.

After a group of high school and college students from our church spent a summer on the field with the Dyes, they returned with exciting reports of God's obvious presence in that home, among their family members, and in the entire realm of the Dyes' ministry.

Paul flew our young people in to the very airstrip where he and Steve Estelle were later ambushed. They met some of the very Indians who would soon "stick their necks out" before the guerrillas pleading for Steve Estelle and Tim and Bunny Cain. Those young people returned, having been infected with the germs of godly enthusiasm. They will never be the same!

It pleases me greatly to know that these missionaries' recent brush with death has been recorded for all to read. I am persuaded that this publication will be like those ancient altars of stone in biblical days, representing a memorial to this generation and those yet future that the Lord "is able to do exceeding abundantly beyond all that we ask or think, according to the power that works within us" (Ephesians 3:20).

There was a time in my life when I picked up and read a book much like this one, and my whole perspective on life was changed. May your experience be similar to mine as you read these pages. Our world could stand a lot more people like Paul and his three fellow hostages. May their tribe increase! And when it does, may God get all the glory.

Chuck Swindoll
Pastor, Radio Bible Teacher, Author
Fullerton, California

Contents

In a city of Colombia, South America, a missionary was talking with two plainclothes marxist guerrillas, one of whom he had known as a civilian. As though intending to be a help to missionaries in tribal areas, the second guerrilla volunteered, "The only solution for you missionaries is to establish relations with the guerrilla commandership so that you can stay at your post."

The missionary understood too well what he meant by such a relationship: Peaceful co-existence, with the guerrillas calling the shots! Though there are many guerrilla groups, all are intertwined toward one objective--the takeover of the Colombian government for the communists.

Then the same guerrilla added, with a firmness that was menacing, "...because *we will win!*"

1

All in an Indian Village

Several boatloads of happy Indians were traveling home from a church conference a while before the trouble started. Each man had his family, in-laws, and pets loaded into a dugout canoe equipped with an outboard motor. Home, to them, was the village of Morichal on the upper Inirida River of Colombia, South America, not too far above the equator.

These Puinave Indians had been meeting with other church groups from many villages. Sometimes such conferences were more like social get-togethers which just replaced the former wild parties of their culture. But this time they had with them a Bible teacher, Tim Cain of New Tribes Mission, who did not have to speak through an interpreter. How different to hear the Bible expounded in their own language! Tim had been the answer to their request for "someone to live with them and teach them more of the Bible." By now, he had lived six months among them, teaching night after night.

Part way home, Tim saw a large boat parked along the bank of the river. It was full of gasoline barrels and manned by about ten Colombians who were strangers to this area. Tim did not think there was anything too unusual about the situation since he knew that drug traffickers sought out the most remote places for the "farming" of their cocaine. And who but drug traffickers would have that much gasoline to sell? (Gasoline was used with alum to prepare the *coca* leaves for making the drug.)

Some of the Indians stopped to buy gasoline for their motors. The boat that was taking Tim, however, was manned by Alberto, captain of the village, and did not stop. Alberto seemed to want to hurry by.

About a month later, Alberto had a little confession to make to Tim.

"Do you remember those ten men who were handling that boatload of gasoline when we came home from conference?" Alberto asked him.

Morichal, the Puinave village, housed about 90 people and frequent guests. The communal building served as dining hall and guest house during conferences.

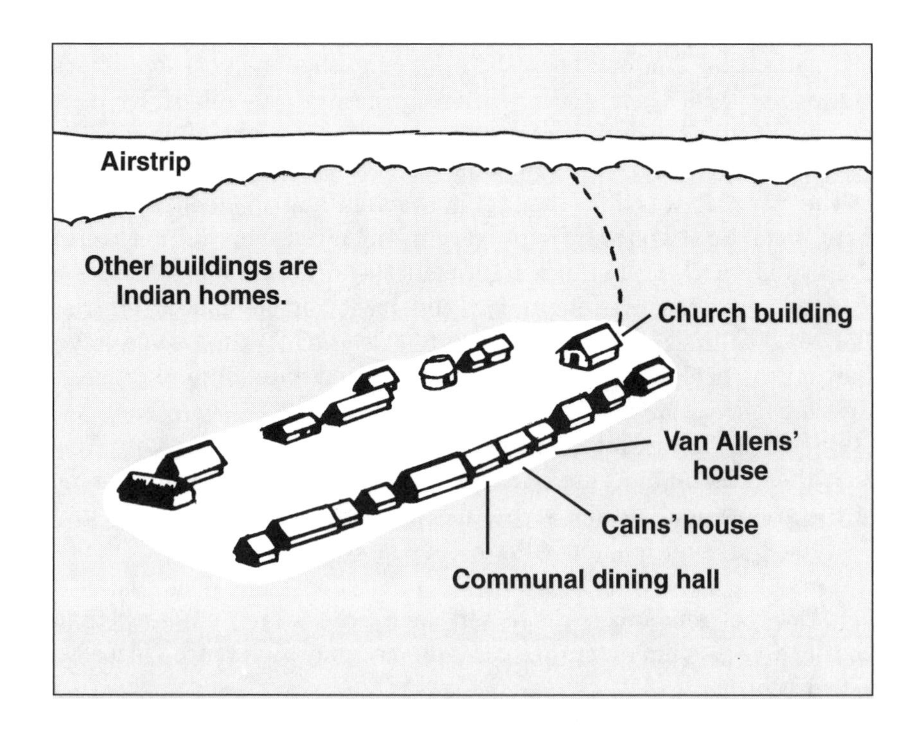

Tim and Bunny Cain with Tina and Cambie

"Yes," replied Tim. "Why?"

"Because there's something I didn't want to tell you at that time. Those men were guerrillas!" Alberto said.

Tim's eyes opened wide. "They were? Why didn't you tell me *then?*"

"Because I thought you would be afraid when you saw guerrillas so near, and you would go away without teaching us any more!" Alberto confessed. He knew Tim had never been that close to a guerrilla.

From the time Tim and his wife Bunny (nickname for Bonnie) had gone into Morichal to teach the Puinaves, they had heard tales of the proximity of the guerrillas. But they were convinced that God wanted them to stay there and lay a good foundation in the Scripture with these people who had heard a lot of truth but were not true believers. They had been reached through Indians of another tribe and had some of the external signs of Christian church-goers, but nothing had dislodged their old beliefs.

Tim had grown up in a place where his parents worked near other Puinaves and was well acquainted with their culture. Then, as a missionary himself, he had spent time downriver learning the language from a linguist-translator who had preceded him into the tribe. Thus, when he entered Morichal, he spoke only in Puinave,

Bunny helps her daughters when they are home.

quickly gaining a rapport with the villagers. Yes, it would take more than a scare to send the Cains home.

In October of 1984, Alberto and another Puinave leader, Chicho, went to the Cains' house — one that the Puinaves had built for them, differing from the Puinave houses only by the addition of windows and partitions. They had an urgent message for the Cains that day.

"Do not go out of your house after dark tonight!" they said to Tim and Bunny, very firmly. "The guerrillas are around. Someone has seen their tracks and their cigarette butts, and it appears there are about eight of them."

Tim and Bunny heeded the warning. The Indians accompanied them to the nightly meeting and back, and they went to bed early. However, there was little the Cains could do to keep a guerrilla from casing the place. Their windows were mere squares in the walls where no mud had been plastered into the lattice-like framework. Screening had been added but no frames, shutters, or blinds.

The following day an older Indian, Anibal, came upon a guerrilla while out hunting. The guerrilla made signs with his hands not to come any closer and to keep quiet. No doubt the guerrillas' camping spot was nearby. The Puinave man turned and left.

Two days later, Chicho was huddled down under a bundle of wild banana leaves in a downpour. As he waited there by the airstrip, he saw eight armed guerrillas walk across the strip from the village side and disappear into the jungle. Each night during that week, the fifty or so dogs of the village kept the villagers well informed of the presence of strangers by their loud yapping and growling.

One night during that time, Alberto's brother felt brave enough to go hunting in his canoe along the riverbank. On his way home, he was stopped at gunpoint, and his game was taken away from him. The guerrillas thanked him kindly for his generosity!

Tim was setting out for the jungle one day to get more poles for the outhouse he was building. Alberto called him back.

"Why are you going out there?"

Tim explained.

"No, you're not!" By this time, Alberto liked to think of Tim as his son in everyday affairs but his teacher in spiritual things.

Alberto called the village together and explained what Tim needed. Tim was to say how many poles and what kind, but in no way would they allow him in the jungle.

During the week, the guerrillas had taken several chickens and had eaten some things out of the Puinaves' gardens. When they met individuals outside the village during the day, they made it known that they were looking for teenage boys and girls to join them. This did not go over well with the Puinaves. Neither the parents nor the young people were interested, but they did not show the guerrillas their true feelings, and not many of them were conversant enough in Spanish to talk further.

One of those whom they questioned was Alberto. In particular, they asked him about the missionaries.

"Just don't worry about them," said Alberto, suspecting that their interest might lead to foul play. "Leave them alone."

There were later episodes of outsiders spending weeks and months in the village. Twice they claimed they were ex-guerrillas, having run away from some guerrilla camp. One never knew for sure whether or not to believe them.

At times when Tim and Bunny were not in the village, strange groups of men came to the village claiming to be cocaine workers. But they carried weapons which only guerrillas used. The Indians told Tim that the strangers had asked about the foreigners again, but that they had always responded with, "Leave those missionaries alone!"

Around the middle of August 1985, Tim and Bunny spent a brief time away from the village and flew back to find the Indians excited over the latest happening in Morichal. Thirty-five guerrillas had appeared in the village, carrying only hand guns, and twelve of them spent the night there. They asked specifically about the missionaries; then left the following morning. The Cains returned just after noon, a safe six hours later.

Given this news at the airstrip, the Mission pilot looked seriously at Tim.

"Tim, don't you think it's getting too dangerous around here? Should we, as a Mission, pull out? I believe the time is coming when we are going to have to face them."

Tim replied, "Oh, I can't leave this infant church now! They're really catching on beautifully. At least, we know now who are believers and who are not; and those who are not want special studies also. I feel so sure God wants me here that I know He'll take care of me." And Bunny, behind him, echoed the same.

Tim was beginning to see an answer to a prayer request of his. He had prayed in particular for some who seemed rather wishy-washy in their profession of Christianity. "Lord, won't You bring about something that will make these people stand up and be counted as Your people," he prayed. "Please shake them up, Lord!" So he was thrilled every time he sensed life in them as far as their walk with God was concerned.

Sometimes the new Christians expressed themselves beautifully in a meeting, either before or after Tim's Bible study with them. For one thing, blessings that formerly they would have ascribed to natural causes or witchcraft, they now attributed to God.

During a meeting in September 1985, for instance, the expressions of gratefulness were more abundant than usual. The Morichal church was to host a conference of other villages and depended on God to supply game to feed the guests. In a dramatic pig hunt, the villagers came in with thirty pigs — in good time for the conference. The Sunday morning expressions of praise ran like this:

> Alberto: "I was just asking God yesterday morning for some game. Well, I was coming home from checking my fish traps with just a few fish and a monkey when I heard shotguns...I knew in my

heart they were shooting at wild pigs. I came as fast as I could. I only had three shotgun shells and soon I had shot three pigs. I ran back to the house to reload my shotgun many times. If I hadn't already been convinced that God answers prayer, I would be now!"

Chicho: "Yes, God sent those pigs! He knows we need them! He sent them right to our village. We didn't need to go looking for them."

Felix: "Just think — He watched over those pigs until we needed them. He did a good job, too, because they sure are fat! And another thing, we were all close enough to get there in time to help."

Anibal: "Those pigs just went around and around in a big circle — just going from one hunter to another, and we didn't have very far to carry them to the village. God thinks of everything, doesn't He!"

Through all the sharing, Tim just sat back and enjoyed himself, listening to these ex-sorcerers and revenge killers as they gave the praise to God!

Someone else had been sitting in on the sharing during that Sunday morning but could not understand more than a few words and phrases of that difficult tonal language. Bob Van Allen and his wife Linda had joined Tim and Bunny as partners a couple of months earlier. They had been given an adobe house with thatched roof right next to the Cains' house.

On his arrival in Morichal, Bob had announced to the Cains, "This is our last move!"

The Cains understood. Bob had been part of a team seeking friendly contact with another tribe when that work was suddenly aborted. Next, he had gone with another missionary to work in a second tribe shortly before guerrillas took over there. In that case, the Indians had hidden him and the other missionary and had helped them escape. Now Bob came to the Puinaves ready to go to work!

However, a freak accident changed things temporarily for the Van Allens. Bob stood up too suddenly in the little loft of a storage area back of his house and knocked himself dizzy on the knot of a rough log. To his wife, a professional nurse, it seemed Bob had a concussion. His blood pressure went off kilter, nausea continued, and, to their great regret, they felt they must call the Mission plane. It came and took them with their three little girls to Villavicencio where there was a doctor.

That was October 2, 1985.

On October 4, Tim was sick and lying in a hammock in the room where his two daughters slept when home from school. His illness had not responded to malarial medicine, and now he was suspecting filaria because of the telltale swollen legs, the itching, and the low-grade fever.

Bunny had been trying to memorize some Puinave phrases from the tape recorder — ever trying to become more fluent in the language. But she needed a break from earphones and from the phrases that were "going round and round" in her head. So she stood up to stretch.

Just at that moment, Bunny looked out the window in time to see a strange Colombian heading for their house on the run. She knew instantly that this man was a guerrilla, though she had never knowingly seen one. He was in camouflage uniform, and, worse than that, he was heavily armed. A belt of huge bullets around his waist intensified the grimness of the outfit. Judging by the determined look on his face, there was no question but that he was prepared to use one of those guns or a hand grenade if offered any resistance. Then she saw another and another — no, four guerrillas!

Bunny just about crumbled right there. She ran into the bedroom. "Guerrillas, Tim! What do we do?"

"Well, go let them in," Tim answered in his matter-of-fact way, still lying down.

"What? No! We don't want them in here!" Bunny knew too much about guerrillas to feel comfortable about inviting them in.

"Just calm down!" Tim said. "We don't even know what they want yet."

Tim climbed out of his hammock, his legs throbbing. By the time he reached the front door, four guerrillas were pounding on it, demanding entrance. Tim opened the door.

"Hands up! And get outside!" one of the guerrillas ordered.

What do you do when four guerrillas point their weapons at you and order you outside? Tim and Bunny obliged. Two other guerrillas were walking around trying to find out who all were in the village. These two also arrived presently at the Cains' house. Another three were out on the river claiming a portion of it as their territory.

Seeing only two missionaries, the spokesman asked, "Where are the others?"

The Puinaves were usually at the airstrip when the plane came.

"We're the only ones here," answered Tim.

"No! There have got to be more!"

"No," Tim contradicted. "You can check and see for yourself. Our partners have left."

They went into the house, made a quick check, and were forced to believe that Tim had told the truth.

"Where did they go?" they asked, characteristically prying.

"Well, our partners left because the husband had an accident and had to go out for medical help."

At first, the guerrillas did not believe Tim. But apparently they got verification from the Indians, for they soon dropped the pursuit of the Van Allens. Then three of them remained outside guarding Tim and Bunny while three others made themselves at home inside the house, going through the Cains' belongings.

It had rained before noon, and the ground was still wet where Tim and Bunny stood all this time with their hands in the air — Tim minus his shoes. It was not the best situation for a sick man. Gathering a bit of nerve, Bunny asked, "Can my husband please sit down? He's sick."

"Oh sure," they said. "He can sit right over here, next to the house." Both Tim and Bunny sat down, a trifle relaxed, and did not put their hands up again. But the guns remained pointed at them — one a machine gun.

The guerrillas had a little consultation among themselves and decided to bring the two missionaries inside, away from the view of any Indians who might pass by. Tim returned to his hammock, and Bunny was seated nearby.

"You have now been detained by the F.A.R.C.," the spokesman announced with an air of importance. (The F.A.R.C., the *Fuerzas Armadas Revolucionarias de Colombia*, is one of Colombia's many Marxist guerrilla groups.)

"Well, what does that mean?" asked Tim, flatly.

"We'll explain that to you later."

Busily, the guerrillas started bringing the Cains' belongings out and making Tim open everything, beginning with the culture file and the language file.

"Now what's this?" they asked. "And what's this?"

Tim and Bunny tried to answer as best they could. The guerrillas continued their search of the house, opening boxes, asking questions, making Tim and Bunny open containers. On the way through that little house, the intruders snatched up anything they felt like taking: food, radio, tape recorderof — even what little cash Tim had on hand. By the time they were through with every shelf, tin, and box, the house was a shambles.

The guerrillas then tried to get into the Van Allens' house next door but could not open the padlock. One of them went back around to the Cains' front door and motioned to Bunny.

"Come with me and open up that house," he ordered her.

Bunny was shaken. Let those vandals into Van Allens' house, too? And what might they *not* do with her away from Tim? She looked over at her husband.

"You can go," he said.

Bunny went over, unlocked, and opened the door.

"Who lives here?" the guerrilla asked.

"Our partners."

"Do they have children?" He was looking at little girls' dresses neatly hung on a crossbar in one corner. The house had only one partition, so this living room also served as the girls' bedroom and the parents' study room.

"Yes, they do." Bunny only answered what she was asked. "Now may I return to my husband?"

"You may," the guerrilla answered.

Bunny walked back, outwardly cool but inwardly shaking and wanting to run to where Tim was. She was relieved and thankful for God's protection.

After approximately fifteen minutes, the same guerrilla came back from the Van Allens' house and ordered Bunny to go back with him again. Again Bunny waited for a go-ahead signal from Tim. "You'll have to go," Tim said.

The guerrilla led Bunny back. Apparently he had locked himself out.

"Open that door again," he ordered. Bunny complied.

"Go on inside!"

Two other guerrillas were standing behind the spokesman, meaning to follow him as he followed Bunny. This was almost too much for Bunny. No Tim at hand to give reassurance. She found herself trembling, convinced by now that this was the end for her. But what choice did she have? The guns were turned on her with every order. So she went in, and all three followed.

"What do you want?" Bunny had found her voice.

"Open up all those containers," they said. "Take off the lids, and tell us what is in them."

Linda Van Allen had carefully stored all her staples in tins that would keep out the humidity and the bugs. So Bunny had to satisfy their curiosity, stating what to her seemed obvious: "flour, cornmeal, rice...."

The kitchen inventory complete, they sent Bunny to the living room. There they began asking about other items in the Van Allens' house: "What's this? What do they use this for?" with the radio, the tape recorder, and on and on. The other guerrillas were doing with the Van Allens' belongings what they had done with Cains'. They took everything out and threw aside haphazardly anything they did not want, taking for themselves whatever they pleased. They seemed quite suspicious about the tape recorder which Linda had been using for her Spanish lessons.

"What's all this about?" they asked, trying to figure some meaning behind the situational dialogues.

"Those are Spanish lessons to help the wife learn Spanish better."

The guerrillas climbed up into the little loft where Bob and Linda slept and ransacked everything there, also. By this time, Bunny asked if she could return to Tim.

"No, you just wait here," they told her.

At this point, another guerrilla came in angrily and started hurling accusations at Bunny in a super-speed Spanish. Bunny knew she was missing parts of what he said.

"Please wait a minute," she requested, "till I get my husband."

"Go ahead!"

When Tim appeared, the guerrilla spokesman resumed his ranting. In effect, he was now answering Tim's earlier question as to what was meant by being "detained by the F.A.R.C."

"You people are Americans," he yelled, "and as such you must be connected with the American government in some way. No doubt you're spies. We are going to see to it that all Americans get out of the country, and the sooner, the better!"

He then added some very antagonistic remarks against Americans in general, concluding, "We're going to begin with *you!* We'll get you out right now!" He paused.

"Go on back to your house!" he ordered.

The guerrillas held another private consultation among themselves. Soon the spokesman addressed Tim.

"Get on the radio, and call the plane out. We want you to say exactly what we tell you to say, and if you change one word, you're dead!"

It was about time for the daily radio schedule, so they forced Tim to call. "Tell them that you're very sick and that you need to go out."

Tim was thinking fast. He shrank from calling the plane at *any* time, let alone now! He did not want the plane to come to this danger spot. However, he *knew* the pilot would buzz the village first to look for a signal to land. Long ago, it had been agreed that either the missionaries or the Indians would wave to the plane as a signal that all was safe for a landing. Tim had trained the Indians well, so he felt confident they would not wave at all this time. Then, too, calling the plane would be the only way to let the Mission know what was going on in Morichal. Besides, there was the guerrilla spokesman reiterating his order and adding, "or we'll feed you to the buzzards."

So at gunpoint, Tim requested the Mission plane to come out the next day, October 5.

Bunny's insides were churning as though something were eating at her from within. The only way to alleviate an awful feeling of weakness was to find comfort in God's Word. There was real relief there. Further, it was a consolation that she and Tim were in on this captivity together.

At suppertime, the guerrillas did their own cooking at the Van Allens' house. Bunny was left to make the most of her tangled house and to fix supper for herself and Tim. But neither of them felt like eating. Tim shared some of his thoughts with Bunny. Cool-headed as he appeared, there was confusion in his mind as to why God would allow the guerrillas to seize them, when their staying on with the little Puinave church had seemed to be under God's direct leading.

In silent prayer, Tim found himself saying, "God, what happened? I was trusting in You to keep these people away from us." Tim's sickness accentuated his feeling of helplessness. Had God betrayed them? he wondered.

Tim and Bunny were grateful to be allowed to stay in their own home and to have their Bibles. Furthermore, they thanked God that their two girls were safe in school and that the Van Allens had left just in time. They were all at the *finca,* or ranch, as the Mission property was called, a few miles from the town of Villavicencio. The *finca* housed the school for missionaries' children, besides the plane and its hangar.

But as for themselves, all was uncertainty. Would a ransom be requested? If so, they had agreed with the Mission that no one should pay a ransom for them. Nor would they have it otherwise. So undoubtedly death was the only answer.

One verse that stood out in their minds meant more to them that evening than it ever had before:

> *"...we know that all things work together for good to them that love God, to them who are the called according to his purpose"* (Romans 8:28).

They kept saying the verse over and over, to themselves and to each other, and dwelling on the truth of it. They declared, "We don't understand it, but we believe it. God *is* in control."

The two went to bed fully dressed that night with their arms around each other. Bunny was shaking uncontrollably for a while. But finally sleep came.

The sleep was a fitful one, however. Every ten to fifteen minutes throughout the night a guerrilla shone his big flashlight on them — right in their eyes — to be sure they were not trying to escape.

The following morning Tim and Bunny faced a dismal shut-in atmosphere. The only break they could look forward to was the coming of the plane. It would fly over the village and the pilot would see the Indians with their arms down and would know it was dangerous to land. This, added to the fact that Bunny was not monitoring the radio as usual, should give indication that something was wrong and that they had not called the plane of their own accord.

While they waited for the plane, the guerrillas picked up the interrogation where they had left off the day before: "Do you have a father here in Colombia? a mother?" "How many brothers and sisters do you have?" "Where are they?" "Does your Mission have people in Villavicencio?" Knowing what could be behind the guerrillas' interest in their affairs, Tim and Bunny were not quick to

The Morichal village common

answer. They tried to be as vague as they could without telling any lies.

The interrogating went on: "What are your people doing in Fusagasugá. (the Mission training school for Colombian missionaries-to-be)?" "How many weapons do they have?" "Why are you here?" "How do you help the Indians?" "Have you ever been to California?" Tim had no idea what California had to do with them or the Mission.

Soon the guerrillas began talking of the plane. It was clear they had designs on it. They had asked Tim when he could expect it at the earliest. Ten minutes before that hour, one of the guerrillas spoke to the others.

"You'd better get going down to the airstrip and be ready!" Clearly, something had been all plotted out. Four of the six guerrillas took off down the path toward the airstrip and soon disappeared from view.

2

Ambush!

Paul Dye, senior pilot for the Mission, is the son of Cecil Dye, one of five martyrs in Bolivia who attempted to reach the Ayoré tribe in 1943.* Paul's first experiences as a tribal missionary had been in Venezuela. Then followed over three years of flying for the Mission in Panama until he answered a request for a pilot in Colombia. Now, after five-and-one-half years of flying in Colombia, Paul and his family looked forward to a long-overdue furlough.

On Friday, October 4, when Tim Cain had called in for a flight, the message was immediately relayed to Paul. Knowing that Tim had not been feeling well, no one marveled that he should have to give in and call for a plane. The radio operator, however, was Tim's mother, Mary Cain. Mary wondered why Tim himself had called since Bunny had been keeping up the radio contact ever since Tim's illness. But Mary did not express all her thoughts at that time. She had to know if Paul would go the following day in order to advise Tim and Bunny.

"Sure we'll go," Paul said, mentally chalking it up to more experience for the new pilot, Steve Estelle. Steve also was a second-generation missionary whose father is vice-chairman of TAC (Tribal Air/Communications), the air arm of the Mission. Paul knew that Tim would not lightly order that two-and-one-quarter hour trip to Morichal, especially since Saturdays were usually "catch-up" days for the pilots. Paul's immediate thought was to take Steve as he had been doing on recent trips, and Steve agreed to go.

Later that night, however, Paul was having some afterthoughts. Now that Steve had received his temporary license for Colombia, perhaps he ought to let Steve fly the little Cessna 185 all alone.

* Their story is told in *God Planted Five Seeds*, also by Jean Dye Johnson.

Paul Dye with the Cessna 185

I've checked him out on that runway, Paul said to himself, and he has done a real good job. That's not the easiest runway to land on — like a roller coaster — and he still did well.

Toward morning Paul sensed God's leading: "No, Paul, go with him — just one more time."

Content that this was what he should do, Paul prepared to "just ride along." I won't say anything to him, he thought. I'm just going to observe on this trip. So Paul prepared to take his Bible and some notes he wanted to study. I'm going to relax, slide my seat back, and just let him go at it, he told himself.

Steve, however, was having some different afterthoughts. For the first time since his arrival as a pilot in Colombia (his previous term in Colombia had not been in the role of pilot), he did not want to fly. He was tired after recent medical exams and after taking his pilot's exam in Spanish. Besides, he had spent much time away from his family flying with Paul. His older son wanted Dad's help with a fort, and his daughter with a dollhouse, especially since her birthday was just around the corner.

On Saturday morning, when Steve was getting things together for the flight, he wondered what was ailing him. He had always wanted to get involved, especially on a medical flight. He knew, too, that Tim was sick and needed the plane; yet, there was a strange feeling in his stomach that he could not explain. As he climbed into the plane, he saw Bill Post, one of the Mission's veteran pilots who was visiting the *finca*. It flashed through his mind, I'll bet Bill would like to go along on this flight. He paused and almost said aloud, "Paul, why don't you take Bill instead of me?"

Steve's sense of duty won out, however. He felt that God was telling him, "Steve, this is your job. You need to learn all of these routes as well as you can and fly with Paul whenever you can." Steve reminded himself that it was for the benefit of the whole Mission there in Colombia that he take advantage of Paul's experience.

The weather was beautiful that morning, and the two pilots sailed right along, Paul enjoying his Bible and notes as he prepared to teach a Bible study at home that afternoon. On the way to Morichal, they made a routine stop at *La Laguna* where the wild Macú Indians were trusting the missionaries more and more. Both Steve and Paul had an avid interest in the progress of the Macú work since each of them had been in on the earlier attempts to gain the friendship of these nomads.

While on the ground there in Macú-land, Tim came on the radio, most unexpectedly, and very much out-of-character:

"When will you be here, Paul?" Even his voice sounded sick. Tim knew the route and had never before asked such a question during a flight.

Mike Gleaves, one of the missionaries to the Macú, was handling the radio. He felt something must have gone wrong with Tim.

"Say, you'd better buzz the village before you land there," he remarked to Paul.

Before leaving *La Laguna,* the pilots loaded on several cardboard boxes of lemons for the school and put another ten gallons of gas in the tanks. They might need a little extra for an airdrop they were to make before going on to pick up the Cains in Morichal.

As Steve flew away from *La Laguna,* Paul prepared to make the airdrop — mail and food — to his son Larry who was visiting with Rich Hess, Gleaves' partner, and the Macús some distance inland. Larry had finished high school and was getting a taste of pioneer missionary work before furlough time for the family. Both Steve and Paul were surprised to find Larry and Rich out in the clearing where the missionaries had been making a garden with the Macú. The airdrop was easy, then, and took no extra gas to find them. Paul was to pick Larry up in a couple of weeks back at *La Laguna*.

Morichal was only forty-five minutes' flight from *La Laguna*. Paul had returned to his special study notes on the chronological or panoramic teaching of the Bible. This was the teaching Tim had given the Puinaves, to which they had responded so well. Paul looked forward now to hearing the latest report from Tim.

As the little plane was nearing Morichal, Steve drew Paul's attention to a thunderstorm which appeared to be moving in on that jungle airstrip. It was a solid, big black wall with lightning, thunder, and strong winds. The palm trees were bowing and bending under the force of the storm.

Steve began to wonder if he could even land. Would he have to turn around and go back? Yet thinking of Tim being so sick, it seemed they ought to try.

Paul took in the whole situation and saw that they were going to have to land with a tail-wind. He put down his Bible and notes and slid his seat up ready to help, if necessary, since the plane had dual controls. This unexpected storm could mean an emergency.

"Just buzz the strip and make sure it's clear," Paul said, thinking of dogs, firewood, or baskets which women often left on the runway.

"Steve, you're going to have to put into practice everything you've learned on this one," Paul added.

Steve started to question, "Paul, *land*? Maybe we should check the village." But he said nothing aloud. No, he's the senior pilot. We're going to land this thing.

In a moment the plane began bouncing in turbulence while Steve kept a firm grip on the controls, guiding it into final approach. Another few gusts and Steve was grateful for the overgrown grass of the runway to help brake it on set-down.

Paul commended Steve for the neat landing he had made in spite of the rough wind and difficult runway. They began to taxi back to the trail which led to the village.

"Man, this doesn't feel right," Paul remarked, not seeing any Indians around where they usually parked the plane. No sign of the Cains either, in spite of the radio call made en route. The Indians must surely be helping Tim close up the house. Perhaps Tim would need help even to walk to the airstrip.

Steve swung the tail of the airplane around and was shutting off the engine as Paul said again, "Steve, something doesn't seem right to me. There's nobody here."

"Here they come!" Steve announced.

Paul looked under the right wing down the trail to where people normally came, and said, "I don't see anybody."

"No, the guerrillas!"

Then he saw them. Two were coming toward them from the front, out of the jungle, and two were coming from behind. There was no escape.

Three weeks earlier, as Paul and Steve were busy working in the hangar, Steve had asked Paul, "What would we do if the guerrillas came out? What is our responsibility as far as the plane is concerned?"

Paul's answer was, "Steve, we can't do anything. I have come to the conclusion, and I base my life on this fact that God is not going to allow anything to happen to us that is not for our good. So if the guerrillas get us, we know it's for our own good — banking on Romans 8:28, because we love Him. If I didn't believe that, I would have packed up long ago."

And here they were! The first part of Paul's words came back now like an echo, "Steve, we can't do anything!"

Neither Paul nor Steve had ever come face to face with a guerrilla before, much less an armed one. In the cities, guerrillas look like ordinary people — many of them intellectuals — always about their business, enlisting recruits, gathering information, just obeying the orders of their superiors. But in the small towns of the interior, when there are no police or soldiers to fear, they wear their camouflage or so-called *tigre* uniforms in part or in whole.

These four men looked fearsome, hair disheveled and somewhat long, and they were "armed to the teeth." Hand grenades hung from their belts, and each one had an automatic pistol besides an automatic rifle. One carried a machine gun. As far as Paul and Steve were concerned, they looked like "bad news." Worse than that, these guerrillas appeared to be very nervous and scared themselves. Hadn't they been taught and had it drilled into them that Americans were hateful and vicious?

The pilots removed their helmets.

"All right, get out of the plane!"

The men did as ordered. Paul leaned on the plane.

"Get away from the plane! Hold your hands up!" the same man commanded.

Steve held his hands up. Paul tried to do likewise, but a knot in his stomach had made him literally too weak to lift them up. To himself he said, Buddy, go ahead and shoot if you want; I'm just not going to hold my hands up. Fortunately they didn't make any issue of the matter.

As the pilots moved obediently to get away from the plane, the captors acted more nervous than ever. It seemed that for each step the missionaries took toward them, the guerrillas took another step back. Paul felt that a scared guerrilla might be more dangerous than a calm one!

One of the four terrorists, whom they recognized as an Indian (not a Puinave), climbed into the plane and began a search — ostensibly for arms. He had Steve open the cargo pod but refused Steve's offer of help to unload it. Out came the lemons and out came some cylinders of gas intended for the Cains' cook stove. The pilots could only watch while this man with a submachine gun dumped all their cargo out on the runway.

Meantime, "Are you Americans?" the leader asked.

"Yes," both the pilots answered.

"All right, you're Imperialists and enemies of Colombia."

Paul responded, "That may be what you've heard, but we're not enemies of Colombia." Paul thanked God that his strength had returned.

"All right, we are the F.A.R.C.," he said. "Have you heard of the F.A.R.C.?"

"Yes."

"Okay, we're the F.A.R.C., and from this moment on, you're being detained by us."

They had little choice but to submit when held at gunpoint from every side. They waited for further orders.

"All right, we have a problem," the leader said, "and if you'll help us solve the problem, we'll let you go."

Paul asked him, "What's your problem?"

"We want you to take two of our men over to another airstrip. Does it take two pilots to fly this airplane?"

Steve spoke up quickly, "Well, it makes it a little easier."

Paul's thoughts were chasing each other around in his head: Steve would not want to fly alone with *these* fellows. Besides, he might not know where he was if they told him to fly out of the Mission's normal routes. Further, they probably only wanted the plane and a pilot and would then let the others go. (Paul had figured by this time that the Cains were being detained in their own house right there in the village.) So Paul spoke up.

"Steve is a new pilot here, and I'm the senior pilot, so I'll take the plane."

"All right, you get up in the airplane then."

"Well, where are we going?" Paul asked.

"Look, you help us with this problem we have, and then you can come back."

"But I don't have enough fuel to go and come back and then go back to Villavicencio."

"There are fifteen gallons over in the village."

Fifteen gallons! That was the exact amount that Paul had left with Tim two days earlier on the trip in for the Van Allens. He knew now that the guerrillas had been into Tim's things as the gasoline was not left out in plain sight.

Once again Paul asked, "Where are we going?"

"Never mind where we're going. It's over that way."

"Look, I have to know where we're going to be sure that we have enough fuel."

"How much fuel do you have?"

"About two hours' worth."

"Oh, that's enough. That's plenty." The guerrilla paused. "What about the weather?"

The storm had moved around to the south and had not come over the airstrip, but it was still thundering and lightning. Paul told the man, "It's pretty bad. I don't think it looks very good." Paul wanted at least to see Tim and Bunny to know how they were doing.

"Yeah, it looks like it's going to rain," Steve added.

The guerrilla could see they were trying to stall so he got stern.

"Get up in there. Let's go!" he said, shifting the gun toward Paul.

Paul got up in the airplane, and two guerrillas got in with him. One had him covered with a gun from behind, the other to his right, with the gun barrel touching Paul's side. Paul was just about to reach for his own set of keys in his pocket when a thought came to him — one that he knew God gave him. "Paul, no! Maybe you'll need those keys later on." So he spoke to Steve through the window.

"Steve, I need the keys."

Steve obliged without a word. This little transaction no doubt led the guerrillas to believe that Steve had the only keys to the plane.

Paul put the key in the ignition.

The guerrilla urged Paul on. *"Vamos,"* he said, meaning "Let's go."

"It's normally my habit," Paul said, "to commit the flight into God's hands."

"Vámonos (Let's get going)!"

Paul chose to interpret the *"Vámonos"* to mean "Let's go ahead and pray." He bowed his head and audibly committed the flight to God, committing their lives into His hands, too. No one interrupted.

Outside the window, one of the guerrillas spoke to Steve in surprise.

"He's praying!"

"That's right," Steve responded, assuring him that that was the thing to do.

Steve and Paul's eyes met before they separated. Steve, outside the plane, gave Paul the encouraging "Thumbs up!" and Paul gave Steve a meaningful reassuring look.

"See you later," he said.

As the plane taxied off to the end of the field, Steve made a motion toward the cylinders and boxes of lemons on the runway. "We need to get these things out of the way of the plane for when it takes off," he said, to get permission of the two remaining guerrillas.

The Indian fellow immediately assumed the role of boss, and all three quickly removed the baggage from the runway. They stood watching until the plane was airborne, then the guerrillas prodded Steve on towards the path to the village — some 500 yards from the airstrip.

Steve had time to think on that silent walk to the village. Paul's words now came back to him forcefully, "God is not going to allow anything to happen to us that is not for our good." It was good that he had let this fact sink in ahead of time. Meditating on it now, his mind turned to II Timothy 1:7, *"...God hath not given us the spirit of fear; but of power, and of love, and of a sound mind."*

How he wished he had brought his Bible! He was glad Paul had his in the plane with him. But God brought another comforting Scripture to his mind.

"Thou wilt keep him in perfect peace, whose mind is stayed on thee, because he trusteth in thee" (Isaiah 26:3).

Steve had seen Morichal from the air only — the creek that wound away from the river and separated the airstrip from the village, and the little church at one end of two or three rows of thatched-roof houses. Now seeing it from the ground, it looked less welcoming than he could have imagined. Not an Indian was in sight, but he was anxious to see Tim and Bunny to know how they were doing.

As they neared the village, Steve saw Bunny walking in front of one of the houses. She was pacing in a very limited area with her head lowered. As Steve came closer, she looked up — far from glad to see him. Without a word, she walked back into the house to tell Tim.

Tim and Bunny had heard the plane coming. When it did not circle the village, they could not believe their ears. They were only vaguely conscious of the storm outside and did not connect it as they normally would have as being a threat to the plane. And now the plane had landed! Tim and Bunny both heard it clearly. To say they were shocked was to put it mildly. The Mission plane had been trapped in an ambush!

Tim broke down then and there and cried as Bunny had never seen him cry in their twelve years of marriage. He felt like a traitor to Paul and Steve.

"But Bunny, I could have said 'No' to the guerrillas when they told me to call!"

Bunny tried to console him. "But Honey, you did what you could. Paul and Steve knew all the signals. God must have wanted it this way or He would not have allowed it to happen!"

The two guerrillas were proud to lead Steve into the Cains' house. What a triumph was theirs to have captured a plane and two pilots! Tim and Bunny only hung their heads. Big tears rolled down Tim's face.

"Lord, why did you let them land?" he breathed.

To Steve, now, he put the question.

"Why did you land? Why?" was all Tim could say.

Steve tried to comfort him. "God...God wanted us to land. Don't blame yourself. You gave indications that there was trouble here, Tim. It's not your fault."

All too quickly, Steve was put in a separate room so he could not talk with the Cains. No plane. No Paul. And now the Cains were taken from him. He turned to God for encouragement.

The separation did not last for too many hours, however. The guerrillas had not counted on interference from the Indians. The Puinaves objected to the treatment of Steve whom they knew as a friend of Tim and Bunny.

Tim had been observing the Puinaves as they went to and from the river. The guerrillas considered them quiet Indians, but Tim could tell from their faces that they were restraining anger underneath. They were zealous for Tim and Bunny and could not stand to have them mistreated. Now they spoke up on behalf of Steve.

"You say you're good people, and yet you treat these missionaries like *this?"* the leaders asked the guards. "These are fellow countrymen! They speak the same language. Let them be together!"

Quite meekly, the guerrillas left Steve free to be with the Cains.

The first thing Steve asked for was a Bible. It was great to share with the Cains the verses which had comforted him on the path from the airstrip. Then Steve looked around to see in what ways he could help, for there were times when the guards were more relaxed. He was able to fix the radio so there would be no more calls for planes!

Thinking from a long range point of view, Steve suggested that some types of things should not be on display for guerrilla investigation. With Tim's prompting from the hammock, Steve helped Bunny do away with certain items like address books and pictures that might lead to a harassment of the family. But when it came to his own family pictures, Steve could not bring himself to destroy them. He handed them to Bunny. "You tear these up for me and dispose of them, will you?"

In vain, Steve waited to hear the Cessna return. He wished he could believe the guerrilla's words to Paul, "Then you can come back." But all hope fled when it became dark. He noted that the guards did not seem to expect the plane back at all.

Steve was a real strength to the Cains that night. He passed on to them what God was teaching him — that this whole situation was allowed by God *for their good*. Thus they committed themselves, Paul, their families, and all concerned to God. They were comforted in the knowledge that folks would be praying for them. Their special request for Paul was that he would not blame himself for telling Steve to land the plane.

3

Other Wheels in Motion

Back in Villavicencio, Bob Van Allen was the first to sound any alarm over the plane's delay in returning. He was staying in town for a few days at the Mission guest home. Still not well himself, he was anxious to see his sick partner, Tim. All he could do was listen in to the radio to see if Mary Cain was getting any responses from the pilots. Any communication outside of scheduled hours was forbidden except in cases of emergency.

Bob knew that Paul intended to be back before 4 o'clock that afternoon, as several events were depending on the return of the plane. Men who had been working out at the school for the electric company waited around to be flown back to Villavicencio — a six-minute flight — rather than have someone take them for an hour's drive by road. Then there was a man who waited for a 4 o'clock Bible study with Paul that Saturday afternoon. So by 4:30, Bob had become quite apprehensive.

He looked up the field committee chairman, Macon Hare, Jr., whose office was nearby.

"Paul and Steve ought to have been back before now," he volunteered. "I wonder if something has happened."

Not wanting to be an alarmist, Macon suggested that they give them a little more time. "Let's wait until 5 o'clock."

In her home at the *finca*, Mary had remained resolutely at the radio, from the time the plane left that morning. She could not understand the silence on the part of the plane or the radio in Tim's house in Morichal. There had only been one garbled word shortly after 3 o'clock that afternoon. What could Paul have said? It sounded vaguely like "Levi." At least it did not seem like the dreaded "Joy Ride" which was Paul's prearranged signal for a hijacking. No doubt Paul and Steve had picked up the Cains and were returning when they tried to make contact. Evidently something had gone wrong with the radio.

Steve and Betsy Estelle with Kimberly, Kenny, and Jason

Steve and Betsy Estelle (far right) are getting adjusted to Steve's new role as pilot.

At 5 o'clock: No news.

At 5:30: No news. No radio contact whatsoever.

Macon headed for the airport, knowing he must report to Civil Aeronautics. But the airport offices — usually open until 6 p.m. — were all closed.

At 7:30 p.m.: Nothing! It had been dark now for an hour-and-a-half. Everyone at the *finca* had caught the concern. Either the radio had failed, or something had happened to the plane, or...(a thought that no one wanted to entertain) could they have been ambushed by guerrillas?

That evening Macon called JAARS, the air arm of the Summer Institute of Linguistics (SIL), to ask if they could send a search plane out over Morichal the next day. They agreed to leave early in the morning.

With these arrangements made, Macon called the Mission Headquarters in Sanford, Florida, to report the missing plane with the four missionaries presumed to be on it: Tim and Bunny Cain, Paul Dye, and Steve Estelle.

The immediate response to this news was prayer. Headquarters called relatives of the four missionaries. Relatives called others. A few churches also were notified and joined the Mission in prayer, though not really knowing yet how to pray.

When Steve's wife, Betsy, went to bed that Saturday night, a thought crossed her mind, This is not the first time I have gone to bed thinking I might wake up a widow!

Betsy was reminded of a time back in 1974 before Steve had taken his pilot's training. He was working with other missionary men seeking a contact with the wild Macú far inland. One night, the Macú had turned on them and were attacking the "strong house" — a log house where the missionaries lived. The last word at the end of broadcast time that night had been ominous.

"We don't know if we can hold out until morning or not!"

Now, this fifth of October, 1985, Betsy comforted herself, remembering how the next day Steve was still alive, and all the men had been evacuated out of the area. (After that episode, the missionaries had switched the contact site to *La Laguna*, a lagoon where they were less vulnerable.) She would hope for the best this time, too.

Betsy determined not to say anything to the children until the following day when they would know something from the search plane going in. However, they had been picking up plenty from hearing other adults and children talk. They stayed up later that night and talked it over with their mother.

"You mean the guerrillas might be holding Daddy?" asked nine-year-old Kimberly with tears in her eyes.

But God had been preparing the hearts of the children. They had been reading a book called *All Things — Even Frisky*. It was about a kidnapping and emphasized the teaching of Romans 8:28, *"...we know that all things work together for good to them that love God...."*

Kimberly recapitulated the story for her mother now, then added, "So we know this is all going to work out for good, too." And shortly she was sound asleep.

Down in Morichal, Steve Estelle was having a rough time sleeping. He knew now what Tim and Bunny meant when they said they could hardly sleep with the flashlight in their eyes every ten to fifteen minutes. He was glad when daylight came and the guerrillas quit using the flashlights.

Steve was up quickly from his hammock, ready for whatever the day might bring. Bathroom facilities were quite comfortable there at the Cains' house. It was just a few yards out the back door to the little outhouse Tim had built with the help of the Puinaves — who had never thought of building such a commodity for themselves. If he wanted to bathe, Steve was told that a guerrilla would accompany him to the creek not too far from the house.

Now he wished that he had brought along a change of clothes and a toothbrush as Paul had. Betsy had even suggested the toothbrush.

"Oh no, I don't need my toothbrush."

Betsy had even pushed a bit. "I just thought you might get stuck on some weird airstrip."

Her words came back to him now. Boy! Next time I'm taking a toothbrush with me and a change of clothes! he told himself with a grimace.

That morning, however, Tim furnished him with a toothbrush and offered him, laughingly, a change of clothes. Tim was of stocky build, and Steve very slight. He could get away with Tim's shirt but looked like a snowman in Tim's pants. He would not risk having the guerrillas laugh at him, so he clung to his own sturdy jeans.

From the front door, Steve could see a file of Puinaves going to and coming from the creek. The women carried their water pots, some with a baby in arms, also. The men carried towels, toothbrushes, and toothpaste. Steve was to learn that this was quite a ritual with these Indians, that toothpaste had become an essential commodity and that the morning bath — a minimum washing the sleep out of face, eyes and mouth — marked the beginning of each new day. What was *not* customary, however, was the use of that particular path to the creek. Each family had worn its own little path down to the creek, as had the Cains. Now the Puinaves deliberately used the Cains' path to the creek in order to check on them. Were they all right? What were the guerrillas doing to them? This, of course, delighted Tim and Bunny who felt so hemmed-in and isolated from the people.

Out in the village, other Puinaves were quietly walking around, helping one of their number prepare for a trip. The believers wanted him to go a day's travel downriver to announce to those at Mosquito Creek that there would be no convention the following week. Tim had previously arranged this Bible study get-together for three other groups of Puinaves he was teaching.

The man taking off had to get permission from the guerrillas to travel — a restriction very foreign to an Indian. However, since he asked permission to take his family, this might include a large number. So two dugouts set out that morning, packed high with all the belongings of the family plus nephews, cousins, friends — young people who were not wanting to be coerced into the guerrilla army.

Bunny was taking her time fixing breakfast about 8 o'clock when the sound of an airplane broke the Sunday morning stillness. The guerrillas became nervous, some of them immediately hiding under the trees near the houses. (The thought of either police or army was too much for a rebel terrorist.) The plane circled very high over the village at first, then came lower and continued to circle the village.

In the meantime, Steve identified it as the JAARS helio courier, a plane specialized for jungle airstrips. Undoubtedly it was sent to search for them and for the Cessna. "Oh no!" he groaned. "All we need is another plane!"

Immediately the three captive missionaries began to pray, as Tim and Bunny had the day before, that the plane would not land.

"The Puinaves deliberately used the Cains' path to the creek in order to check on them."

“Make it go away, Lord,” they prayed. “How can we cope with any more problems here.”

Tim, with his swollen legs, his aches, fever, and general malaise still hurt worse over the Cessna’s landing than he had ever hurt physically. Now, more than ever, he pleaded with God, *“Do* make it go away!”

The guerrillas, after some discussion among themselves, interrupted the missionaries’ praying.

“Come on to the airstrip,” they said to Bunny and to Steve. They knew better than to try to include Tim who could hardly walk.

Down the path they started single file: a guerrilla, then Steve, Bunny, and another guerrilla. Walking at a fast clip, the two guerrillas rather carelessly guarded their captives. (Steve at times was more concerned over the casual way they handled their automatics and hand grenades than he was about when they would decide intentionally to shoot the missionaries!) On the way, the lead guerrilla began to instruct Steve as to the role he was to play.

“I want you to make that plane land!” he told Steve. “You do exactly as we say, or we’ll shoot you!” But even as he said it, the plane just kept on going and flew away.

Steve breathed a sigh of relief and felt God had answered their prayer. Everyone stopped there on the path for a few minutes, waiting to see if the plane would return. Not quite knowing what to do, the guerrillas sent Bunny back to the house to be with Tim while they ambled on down to the airstrip with Steve.

There the guerrillas stationed Steve in plain sight on the runway with a white towel from Van Allen’s house. They themselves entered the jungle that lined the sides of the airstrip, and each stood under a tree, well hidden from view, should the plane return. Steve was to wave the towel to try to make the plane land while they stood some twenty to twenty-five meters behind him with guns pointed at his back. Out there in the sun, the bugs made a beeline for Steve.

Then the helio returned. Steve could not believe it. He didn’t know it had merely gone to check another airstrip. Anew he prayed with fervor that it would not land. He found himself very nervous, not wanting their plane and pilots to be in the predicament he was in. But he was getting orders from behind. “Wave that flag!” the guerrillas ordered.

Steve stalled a bit, requesting the exact motions. They were not too sure themselves, having just learned from someone that the waving of a flag was a signal for the Mission plane to land. Steve still had them show him explicitly how to wave it. Then it was his turn.

"Like this?" Steve waved it downwards. "Or like this?" waving it a bit differently.

"Yes, yes," they said. "Just wave it!"

In rather ungainly motions with the towel, Steve waved, looking straight ahead and praying. With his free hand, he batted at the bugs on his neck and throat.

"How am I doing?" he asked the guerrillas, in the midst of his performance.

"Just fine! You're doing great!" They cheered him on, caring only that he waved. They did not know that the flag-waving was *not* a signal for other planes besides those of the New Tribes Mission.

Steve's stiff soldier-like stance did not go unnoticed by the pilots of the helio. Surely he would not wave like that of his own accord. Besides, they had their own orders *not* to land. Finally they swooped down in quite close, flaps down, and it seemed they would land. Steve felt free to quit waving. But they flew on again.

The guerrillas were angry with Steve because the plane did not land. "Why didn't it?" they asked him.

"I don't know," he said. "Maybe because they only saw one foreigner out here."

"Oh no!" they contradicted. "You don't look like a foreigner. You look like a Colombian." (Steve was rather dark complected and of medium height.)

"If it comes back here one more time, I'm going to shoot it down," said one guerrilla. "It's neat to shoot a plane down. I did once."

"But that's a *helio courier!"* Steve exclaimed, groping for a rationale and stalling for time. "It's a special plane. You wouldn't want to shoot it!"

"What is it?" they asked, as the plane made one more pass.

"A he-lio cou-rier." Steve sounded out the English word with a Spanish pronunciation. And by that time, the plane had gone for good.

At 6 a.m. that Sunday morning, October 6, Macon had returned to the airport to report the missing plane. He found that Paul had relayed word by radio (through another pilot) of his landing in Morichal the previous day. The Civil Aeronautics authorities strongly suspected guerrillas.

Macon reported to the American Embassy as he was required to do if any American member of the Mission should be missing. He sought advice from other authorities also. One with whom he spoke was quite optimistic.

"This happens all the time," he said. "They use your plane for a trip and let you go. Your folks will be out this afternoon."

Macon was not so sure.

The Sunday morning service was held as usual at the *finca*. Pat Dye, Paul's wife, was at the piano. Connie Cain, Tim's father, took charge of the meeting. At the end of his message, he shared a verse he had noticed that morning in his Bible reading.

"Know ye that our brother Timothy is set at liberty; with whom, if he come shortly, I will see you" (Hebrews 13:23).

For the first time, tears flowed in public.

Macon's already busy schedule took on new priorities. He must keep in touch with the home end of things constantly. He talked on the phone with members of the Executive Committee in Sanford, Florida, in particular with his father, Macon Hare, Sr., and Mel Wyma, both of missionary experience. They decided together not to inform the media unless it should become necessary.

Al Meehan, one of the two JAARS pilots who had flown the helio over Morichal, flew to Villavicencio to meet with Macon. He asked to see a photograph of Steve Estelle and assured himself that it *was* Steve he had seen on the airstrip at Morichal. How Al would have liked to scoop him up on one of his "fly-by's!" But things could not have looked more abnormal

Al told of the propane bottles and the boxes of green fruit (lemons) that he had seen on the side of the strip. Further, he had seen two canoe-loads of Indians leaving the village. The canoes were packed to the hilt, giving him the impression that the Indians were evacuating. Only at one end of the village had he seen a few Indians huddled low in a hut — so out-of-character for these Puinaves who were usually excited to see the plane.

As for the Cessna, there was no sign of it, even though the helio had flown for a "look-see" over some nearby airstrips. They did not hear the ELT (emergency locator) beacon at any time.

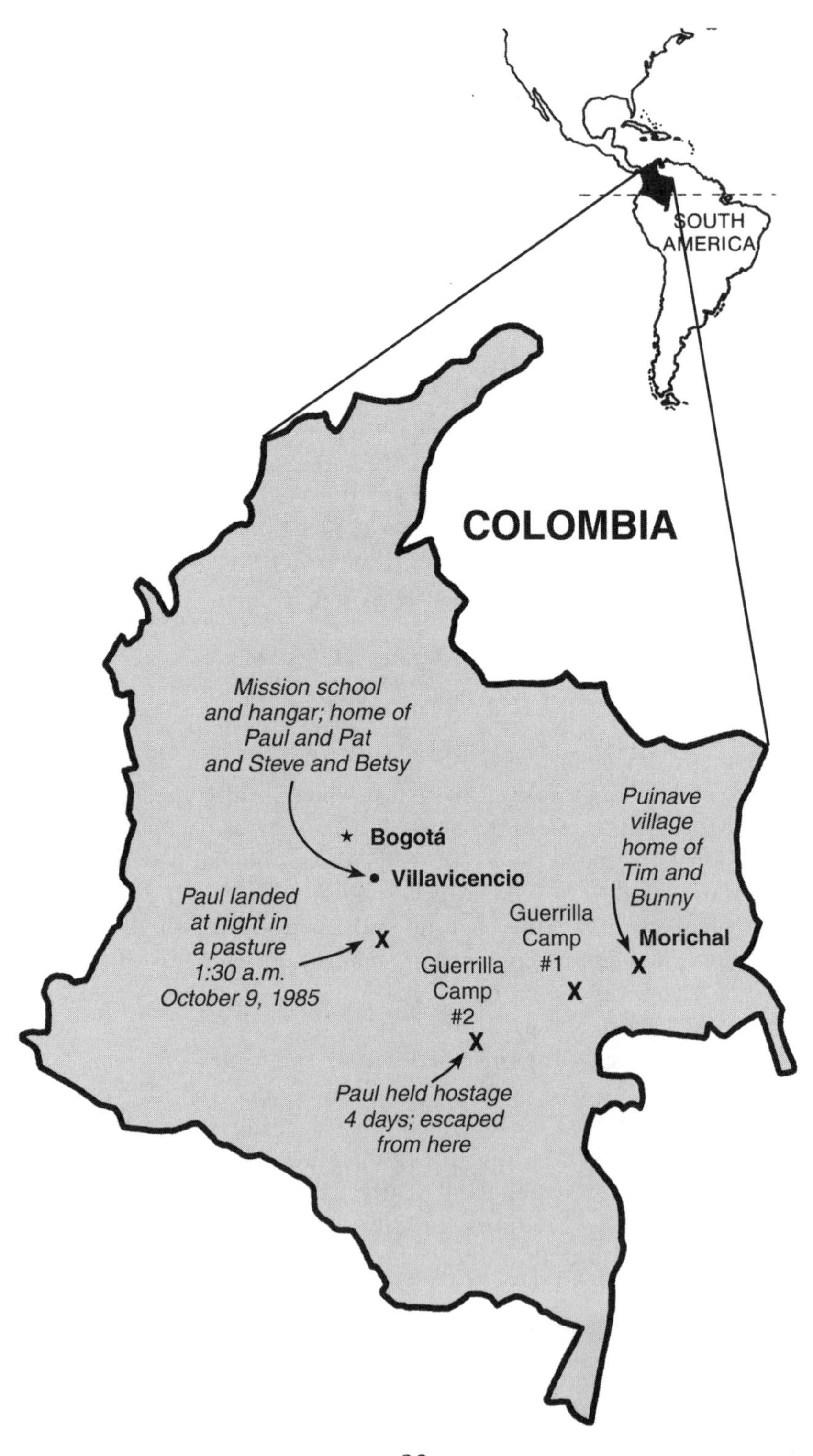
SOUTH AMERICA
COLOMBIA
Mission school and hangar; home of Paul and Pat and Steve and Betsy
Bogotá
Villavicencio
Puinave village home of Tim and Bunny
Morichal
Paul landed at night in a pasture 1:30 a.m. October 9, 1985
Guerrilla Camp #1
Guerrilla Camp #2
Paul held hostage 4 days; escaped from here

Until then, it was presumed that the four were together in the plane. Now there was no doubt in anyone's mind that guerrillas had ambushed the plane and had made Paul fly it away. No doubt the crime would be followed by a ransom note.

Some years before, the Mission had made a firm decision, in agreement with all of its members, that they would never pay ransom for a missionary. The paying of ransom had already snowballed in favor of the guerrillas who sought out ranchers, Americans, or anyone whose families would be wealthy enough to pay.

In January 1981, one group of these Marxist guerrillas had tried to get their way by kidnapping a Bible translator, Chet Bitterman of SIL. Macon was in Bogotá at the time, where the Mission headquarters used to be located. He recalled now the vivid details of Chet's capture as told by some of Chet's companions:

> Chet and his family had been in Bogotá for medical attention. At about 6:30 a.m. on January 19, someone disguised as a policeman knocked at the door of the SIL guest home. When the door opened, six terrorists, hooded and armed with machine guns and revolvers, burst in. All in the house were herded into the living room and made to lie facedown on the floor while the guerrillas tied their hands and feet and gagged them — 12 adults and five children. Mothers and children were seated on the couch.
>
> Apparently frustrated by not finding the director at home, the kidnappers chose Chet. Four days later, the terrorists made their demands:
>
> "Chet Bitterman will be executed unless the Summer Institute of Linguistics and all its members leave Colombia by 6 p.m. February 19."
>
> (signed) M-19, National Coordinator Base.
>
> The Summer Institute of Linguistics had previously made the decision that they would not give in to terrorists. Even the college where Chet graduated agreed that negotiations were impossible. President J. Robertson McQuilkin said, "Once you start giving in to terrorists, you jeopardize every missionary the world over."
>
> An extension of two weeks was granted by the M-19 guerrillas, but on March 7, Chet received the martyr's crown.
>
> (Condensed from a special issue of *In Other Words*, April, 1981)

M-19, however, had not limited its target to the Summer Institute of Linguistics. Any mission having an office or guest home in Bogotá not only prayed for Chet but automatically put itself on guard. In the New Tribes Mission headquarters, all were told never to go to the door without first checking on the visitors through the window.

Macon Hare was working in his third-floor office of the New Tribes Mission headquarters on the night of February 18. He was also often in prayer for Chet, realizing that the original deadline to "execute" (as though murder were a legal execution!) was coming up at 6 p.m. the following day. This, he knew, would be true to form since the M-19 guerrillas like to "do their thing" on the 19th of the month.

Engrossed in his work, Macon did not realize it had passed midnight, from February 18 to February 19, until he heard the doorbell ring. He opened the third-floor window and looked out.

There was a Volkswagen car on the street, and three men were standing at the door. They held up little cards that had F2 written on them.

"We are F2 police," they said, meaning that they belonged to the plainclothes branch of police.

Macon was immediately suspicious. The little cards did not look very official, and the captors of Chet Bitterman had claimed also that they were police.

"What do you want?" Macon asked them.

"We just want to talk to the American," they said. "We have some papers for the American to sign."

"But why at this hour of the night?" asked Macon, still from the third-floor window. In answer, they kept insisting that they just needed him to sign some papers — never giving the name of "the American."

Any credulity Macon might have had at first left him. It was his turn to try one of their tactics and see if he could influence them by fear.

"Katy!" he called to his wife over his shoulder, "Bring the shotgun!" though there was no gun in the house. Then he turned back to the visitors below.

"I'm going to call the police station to check who sent you here," he said.

This caused a restlessness among the three on the street. Their car, with a fourth man at the wheel, was still running.

At this moment, a missionary down on the second floor went sleepily to the window in delayed response to the doorbell. The opening of that window set off a loud burglar alarm that could be heard out on the street.

The three "police" quickly squeezed into the little VW. The car promptly stalled, and the starter did not function. So the three jumped out again and began to push. The last Macon saw of them they had rounded the corner and were still pushing a block away. But by the time the city police came they had managed to get away.

Later on, Macon saw an arrow pointing to the house with M-19 painted under it — a clear sign that they were a marked target.

On March 7 the guerrillas did carry out their threat and murdered Chet Bitterman. This tended to backfire against that Marxist rebel group. The media was in sympathy with SIL and Chet. Nevertheless, M-19 was not through.

In the evening of March 19, a group came again to the New Tribes Mission home. This time Oren and Alma Green were the only missionaries present along with a faithful Colombian secretary, Cecilia. Oren had stepped out for a short time to buy a barbecued chicken — a treat as available as hot dogs in America — when the group came to the door. The two ladies heard them pounding on it but refused to answer. They preferred to give the impression that no one was home.

Meanwhile, a neighbor across the street telephoned Cecilia and described to her what the men were doing at the door. They gave all evidence of being the M-19 group, but after getting no response from within, they took off.

Seconds after they left in their car in one direction, Oren, all unaware, walked back around the corner from the other direction! Needless to say, there was gratefulness for the chicken that night and heartfelt thanksgiving for God's precision timing.

Now, with all the facts he knew, both past and present, Macon had to consider the Cains and the two pilots as "prisoners on death row." For them, there was no way out except by a miracle. He could only ask God to work that miracle. Above all, he asked God to do whatever He would to bring the most glory to Himself. Everyone else there at the *finca* was of like mind in prayer. How it drew them all together!

Folks asked the pilots' wives, Pat and Betsy, what they could do for them. One of the schoolteachers, also a carpenter, volunteered to put together the dollhouse that Steve had wanted to do for his daughter Kimberly's birthday. Luke Dye, twelve, and Jason Estelle, eleven, suddenly became the best of buddies. They had something very much in common — a missing father. The Cain girls, glad to have their grandparents on the school grounds, joined the others in asking God for a miracle release of their parents. The children especially seemed convinced that God knew how to take care of the kidnapped missionaries.

Back in the United States, Canada, and England, parents and relatives contacted other parents and relatives. A chain reaction of prayer began. Students and staff in ten training centers of New Tribes Mission began praying and getting their home churches to pray. Even churches who were not acquainted with the Mission began praying long before the news was given to the media. Any who remembered the story of Chet Bitterman prayed yet more fervently, knowing they were not dealing with mere politics but with real enemies of God — trained to believe in a cause that denied God.

4

Joy Ride

On takeoff with the guerrillas from Morichal, Paul circled over the village to see if he could see Tim and Bunny. But there was no sign of them. Only the Indians stood outside their houses, looking up. Instead of their usual exuberance at the plane flying over, not one of them waved. Paul could hardly bear to see them standing there with their arms hanging down, looking so sad. It certainly was not their fault that he had landed!

An incident flashed through Paul's mind of a "mistaken landing" he had made in another tribe. An Indian had waved for him *not* to land; but Paul interpreted the signal to mean that the coast was clear. He landed. Immediately he sensed that something was wrong. The Indians were making all kinds of contortions with their arms. As Paul was about to turn off the engine, a brave Indian ran up to the plane and clarified what the real excitement was about.

"Keep going! Get away quick! The guerrillas! They're right there just inside the jungle waiting for the plane to stop!" And Paul zoomed off like a shot!

But the Morichal villagers had their signals straight. If only he and Steve had circled the village...!

Now, as Paul headed out in the "over there" direction, one guerrilla asked, "Do you know where the Fulano's airstrip is?"

"Yes, I know where it is."

"Then that's where we want to go."

Paul headed for it in a straight line, and the river was getting farther and farther south. The man got worried. "Where are you taking us?"

"Didn't you want to go to the Fulano's airstrip?" Paul asked.

"Then how come you're going away from the river?"

"Well, it just happens this course cuts straight across," Paul replied. The man continued to worry a bit, then sure enough, he saw the airstrip coming up and was greatly relieved.

At the airstrip where they landed were eight more guerrillas, all uniformed and decked out with guns and hand grenades just as Paul's "passengers" were. The one who had been holding a gun at Paul's back jumped out and went off with the eight guerrillas. The one alongside Paul quickly took the keys away from Paul, got out, and held a gun on him.

"Don't get out of the airplane," he said. "Just stay there."

Soon a lady came out of a house alongside the runway, bringing some cans of beer. She gave one to the guerrilla guarding Paul, then offered a can to Paul.

"No, thanks," Paul responded, "I don't drink beer."

"How about some lemonade?" she volunteered.

Paul gladly accepted. She left, to return in a matter of moments with the lemonade. As she returned again to the house, Paul thought to himself, What is a young lady like that doing in this type of company? She looked like a nice, well-groomed university student. But there she was with the same paraphernalia as the men — guns, hand grenades, camouflage uniform — and probably steeped in the same doctrine.

Paul was thirsty by this time and appreciated the lemonade, but he became concerned about the cans of beer. Oh boy! If these fellows get worse when they're topped off with liquor...He didn't finish the thought. He heard an outboard motor head off upriver.

Paul waited and waited, still with the gun barrel leveled on him.

After about twenty minutes, a motorboat came in from upriver with a guerrilla commander and another woman guerrilla. Both had the regular array of arms over their uniforms. The commander's uniform, however, was a military one, not the usual camouflage. He was slight of build, of medium height, and with somewhat unruly curly hair.

"Hola!" the commander greeted Paul in Spanish. "We want you to make one more flight for us before we let you go."

"Where are we going?" Paul asked. By now he did not believe it when they talked of letting him go. It would be too late in the day to return to Morichal.

"Well, we're going *that* way. I can't tell you where we're going. How much gas do you have on this plane?"

"Well," Paul replied, "I had two hours of gas and have used up half an hour, so I have one-and-a-half hours left." Paul never counted his reserve, and he had long forgotten the extra ten gallons taken on at *La Laguna*.

"Oh, that's plenty!" he assured Paul. With that, the commander got in beside Paul. The same guerrilla who sat behind him on the first leg of the trip climbed in behind Paul again, covering him with his gun. The woman who had come in the boat got in behind the commander.

"OK, let's go!" the commander shouted.

"I'm going to pray first," Paul said, and did so. Amazingly, once again while Paul prayed for the flight, the guerrillas were quiet. Nor was any remark made afterwards.

Soon they were airborne, but Paul needed to know which way to head.

"Look, we'll be flying over the jungle. I have to know where we're going. In which direction?"

"Fly 280 degrees."

Paul started off, as ordered, flying 280 degrees. As the river started getting farther and farther away from the flight path, the commander became worried, just as the former front seat "companion" had done. Both were better acquainted with river transportation than air.

The man pulled out his compass and held it up to the master compass of the plane to see if the two read the same. He did not understand that in an airplane a compass has to be compensated, due to all the metal in its proximity. This was causing his compass to read erroneously. He became disoriented and frustrated.

"Where are you going?" he said.

"I'm going where you said to go — 280 degrees," Paul replied. Then he tried again to get better information.

"Look, man, I am flying this plane; and when we land, I will see where we are going, anyway. So just point out on the map where you want to go, then I can draw a straight line and save gas."

Paul saw that this guerrilla needed to be scared into complying. So he continued, "If we wander all over the jungle, we'll run out of fuel. When that happens, the motor will stop, and this plane'll go down like a rock. Then we'll all die together when we smash into the ground."

Exaggerated or not, the matter finally came across as serious. The commander really got worried and said, "All right." He pointed on the map to a tiny town.

"Is that where you want to go?"

"No," said the commander, "but I want you to go there first."

Paul kept at it since their lives depended on it.

"In other words, go there first and then we'll take another route and go up another way? Just tell me where your destination is, and I'll draw a straight line."

Finally, the commander gave in. He pointed to where two rivers came together and said, "Right there!"

With the use of his plotter, Paul made the calculations. Meantime, they had flown quite a distance. The new heading needed to be 250 degrees instead of 280 — a big difference in jungle flying.

For a while, Paul had been seeking an opportunity to give a low signal on the radio. He felt sure Mary Cain would still be listening in, as she did during all the Mission flights. He tried to say "Joy Ride" — their signal in case of a hijacking — but was forcibly interrupted. The commander saw his lips moving and yanked the cord out of the jack.

"Don't talk to anyone," he ordered, quite upset.

Along the way, the commander asked Paul, "Do you know who we are?"

"No," Paul answered. His original captors had told the identity of their group, but there were so many little terrorist groups. It seemed important to know for sure.

"We belong to the F.A.R.C.," the commander announced. "Have you ever heard of us?"

"Yes, I've heard of the F.A.R.C."

"Well, that's who we are."

What Paul *did* know of the F.A.R.C. was that it was one of a few Marxist groups who had signed a peace treaty with the government. If the government learned of this hijacking, that treaty would be in danger.

The commander went on, "Why are you people afraid of us?"

"Only because of those guns," Paul replied.

"We're good people," was the response. "We're fighting for the peace of our country."

"Oh, you *are*?" from Paul.

Finally, they came within sight of the junction of the two rivers. The commander's face lit up. "Now just fly up this river a bit till you come to an airstrip," he said. Sure enough, within fifteen minutes they came to a jungle strip about 700 meters long.

Paul had been flying quite high all this time, using his navigational aids. It seemed he could touch anything on the panel, and it did not alert the commander. Paul was keeping check on exactly where he was in reference to another airstrip that had a radio navigational aid. As he circled down, he studied the area well before landing. He saw a road at the far end which disappeared into the jungle. "They must have a vehicle here," he made a mental note.

About a third of the way down the runway, there were four half-hidden houses where Paul expected them to have him park since everything else around was jungle. But the commander hurried him on past the houses and past thirteen armed guerrillas who were guarding the runway. Paul was to head for the entrance to that road at the end of the strip. All thirteen of the guerrilla guards followed the plane.

Obeying the commander's instructions, Paul turned left to enter the road. But what a "road" for an airplane! It was crudely cut, perhaps 200 meters long and did not appear to be wide enough for the Cessna.

"Right here," the commander said. "Drive it straight in there, nose into the trees."

Under normal conditions, Paul would never have attempted it. He had been trained to be very meticulous about a plane and had taken excellent care of this one, feeling that it belonged to God for the use of missionaries to the tribes. But certainly, guns behind and beside did not make for "normal conditions." He feared now for the wing tips touching the trees on either side.

"Man," he said, "this won't fit in there!"

"Yes, it will. We've had other planes in there."

"Look, let me shut the engine off and I'll go look first to see if I can get it in."

"OK." The commander took the keys away from Paul and got out. Paul got out, too, and walked on in. He could see it would be a very close fit.

"No, it won't go in there," he concluded, and informed the commander so.

"Yes, it *will* go in there!" And to show he would not stand for any more arguing, he shoved the end of his gun barrel at Paul.

"Get up in the plane and put it in there!" he said.

"OK, I'll do what I can."

So the commander got in behind him with the gun and handed him the keys with a menacing comment, "I'm going to get in here, too. We can't afford to lose this bird now!"

At the end of the 200-meter road, the circular clearing was too tight to turn the plane around. Paul parked it in a way that would keep the wing tips from hitting the trees and turned off the engine before reaching the far end of the road. Then everyone climbed out. But the guerrillas had other ideas for parking the plane. They pushed it on into the woods by hand to make sure it would not be easy to get out. Then the commander spoke to the leader of the guards.

"Look, I'm placing him in your charge, and I want maximum security!" he told him.

"Yes, sir. No problem," the guard answered.

The commander with his lady companion and fellow comrade who had come in the plane left Paul with the guard and headed back toward the airstrip and the houses. The others returned to their work on the runway.

The guard then turned to Paul, "Come on. Let's go."

"Just a minute. May I take my Bible and a change of clothes with me?"

"Sure," said the guard, not unkindly, "bring anything you want."

Paul quickly got his leather folder which protected his Bible and study notes. Also he pulled out his leather bag with a change of clothes. Out of habit, he put in the control lock, secured the Pitot tube cover, and shut the door of the plane. Automatically he wanted to lock the doors, but he remembered in time that he dare not pull his keys out of his pocket to do so. He walked away sadly from the plane.

The guard had been patiently watching and waiting for him. "Follow me," he ordered.

He headed out on a narrow path indicating that Paul should follow him. Paul was surprised that he should be left to walk without a gun pointed at him from behind. But he had long ago been informed that if a prisoner tried to escape from one of those guerrillas, there was one answer, "Shoot to kill!" So he merely took advantage of the walk to look everything over really well and to observe all he could. Occasionally, the guard looked back over his shoulder to see that Paul kept coming. The path led for about 700 meters toward the west, away from the plane and airstrip. It ended at a little camp a few yards from the river.

This camp had not been visible from the air because of the big trees hovering over it. Further, it harbored no houses that might give privacy to either guards or "guests." But there were small shelters. A rope, extended from one tree to another, was sufficient to hold a sheet of plastic. This would ward off the rain over a bed of four boards set up on poles.

There were six such shelters for the guards. Under each piece of plastic was a thin foam mattress and mosquito net to cover the bed, and on each bed was a back pack. This gave the appearance of a camp ready to be abandoned on very short notice. At the edge of the riverbank was a larger temporary shelter used as a kitchen. It boasted a table of poles and a pot strung from the roof down to a fire on the ground. A barrel of water completed the layout. A guerrilla, armed like the others, was there cooking supper as Paul was led in.

Paul's guard stopped in the middle of the camp by his own shelter and turned around to face his captive. He pointed to four boards which lay on the ground by four old gasoline drums, only a few feet away.

"This is yours," he said. "You can sleep here." The guard stepped back to his own bed and began fiddling with a battery tape recorder.

Left to himself temporarily, Paul stood looking at the boards a moment, then dropped his bag on the ground and sat down on it. If only he could wake up from this awful nightmare! But he must keep his mind on urgent matters at the moment. He would have to take immediate action on some of the things he carried with him: In the leather folder with his Bible was the checkbook of the airplane account. Also, he carried a $500 check to pay for fuel he had purchased. It would be too easy for them to find some way to cash it. Further, he had his address book containing phone numbers of friends and relatives. Then there were his documents. He must find some way to destroy anything with information that they could use to their advantage.

First of all, though, his own keys were "burning a hole in his pocket." During moments when the cook and the guard were preoccupied, he took care of the matter of the plane key first. The last time the commander had taken the keys from him, Paul had purposely acted reluctant to surrender them, not wanting him to know

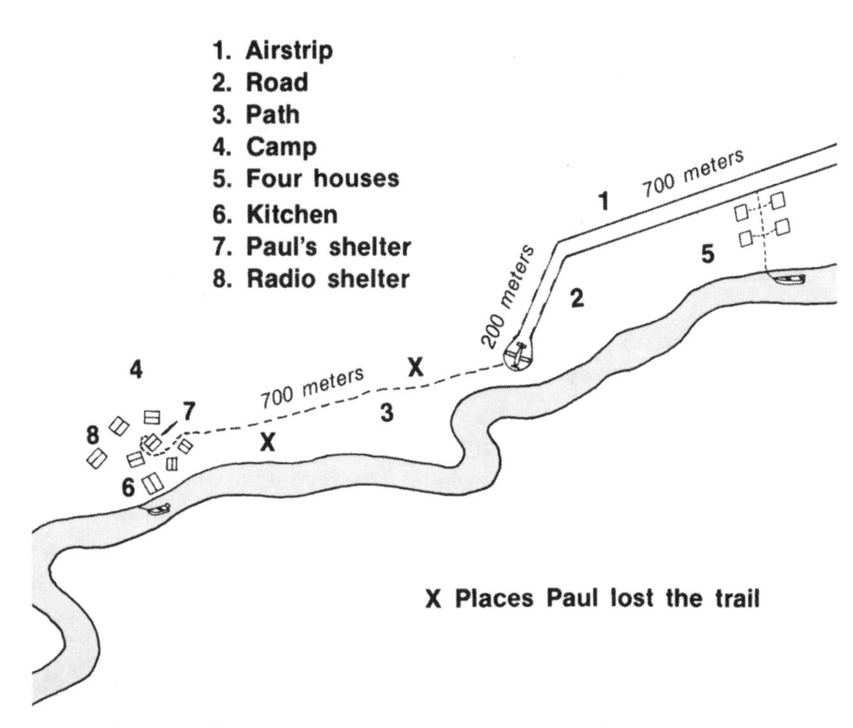

The guerrilla airstrip, road, path, and camp: where Paul took off in the dark and where the trio was led blindfolded

he had the other set of keys. Now Paul removed the ignition key from the keyring. Keeping his eyes on the two guards, he pushed the point of the key deep into the inner lining of his shoe, then slipped the other keys back into his pocket. "Thank you, Lord," he breathed.

Then he gave attention to his address book. It would be rough if these terrorists would use it to harass his relatives or friends. He noticed a pole, three inches in diameter, stuck in the ground nearby. Slowly and carefully he pushed it back and forth, loosening it up. Whenever the guard would look at him, he would pretend that he was just hanging onto the pole. Finally he had it loose and gently pulled it out and laid it on the ground. Then reaching into his back pocket he took the address book, rolled it up and dropped it into the hole. When he had opportunity, he replaced the pole in on top of it. Other things he would have to dispose of after dark.

Now and then, Paul became conscious of the knot in his stomach — the same knot which had seemed to weaken him on his first encounter with the guerrillas. Thinking back now to that ambush, he could not quite believe what had happened. If only he could wake up and find it was all a bad dream! Yet, the reality was so strong he had no choice but to believe it.

Immediately Steve's question that time in the shop came back to mind, "What are we going to do if the guerrillas get us?" Now Paul reviewed his own answer: "I base my life on the fact that God is not going to allow anything to happen to us that is not for our good." Here, confined in the guerrilla camp, he tried to dwell on this thought...for our good...for *my* good.

Suddenly, he heard footsteps coming down the trail to the camp. He looked up to see four more guerrillas arriving. They walked straight over to the kitchen and sat down on a log. Paul's guard, the leader, called one of them over to set up Paul's shelter and bed. He promptly set the four barrels in position on their sides and placed the four boards on top of them. Then he set up the mosquito net and plastic, all without relinquishing his automatic rifle. When all was complete, this guard took time to quietly stare at the new captive for a few minutes before returning to join the rest who were starting to eat supper over at the kitchen.

Soon the cook brought Paul his supper. It consisted of plain rice and macaroni with a plate-size *arepa* (deep-fried cornmeal pancake).

"Here is your food," he said. Paul thanked him. He, too, stood there a while to get a closer look at this six-foot, blonde-haired pilot.

As soon as he left, Paul looked at the food on the plate.

You'd better eat to keep up your strength! he told himself. But the more he looked at the food, the more nauseated he felt, till he could not take a bite. That old knot in his stomach had not left him. He chided himself and tried a piece of the *arepa*, which had sugar instead of salt. But when he saw the grease ooze out of it around his thumb, the nausea increased. He walked over to the kitchen and handed back the untouched plate.

"I'm not hungry," Paul told the young cook — a seventeen-year-old boy.

"That's normal," was the response. "You'll eat after you get used to being here."

Paul did not care for the implication "...get used to being here!"

At least, it had felt good to walk to the kitchen. He was allowed to walk within the circle of shelters but was told that the radio shelter and the path to the plane were both off limits. The river, too, was off limits. If he wanted to take a bath, he must dip water out of the barrel that stood by the kitchen. If he needed to go into the woods, a guard must accompany him the whole time.

"If you violate these boundaries, you will be shot," he was told.

By this time, it began to get dark, and the mosquitoes were biting, so Paul climbed into his mosquito net. Unfortunately, there was nothing underneath him to keep the mosquitoes from entering between the cracks in the boards. He had already detected them to be of the anopheles species. Oh boy! Here comes malaria again! was his mental comment.

Soon the guards began testing their flashlights. It did not take long for Paul to learn why. Every three to five minutes one of them walked up to his net and turned the flashlight on him. Maximum security for sure! He was to find out that the guards were taking two-hour shifts through the night.

By now he was thinking of the documents he still had, so he began to go through them, using the light of his wrist watch to see which ones had current addresses. He became proficient at guessing when the guard on duty would flash his light on him again. Soon he located the check for gas. First he tore it, then chewed it, then buried it in the soft jungle floor under his bunk. Other documents he dropped into the bunghole of one of the barrels holding up his bed. Paul heard them splash into water in the barrel. Before he finished censoring his documents, the battery in his watch gave out. Now he had no light and no way to tell time either. He felt as though everything he had depended on was taken from him!

Paul leveled with himself. I've always taken my liberty for granted, he mused, till I had it taken away from me at gunpoint. What a comfort it was for him to know that, even though they could take away his liberty, they could never separate him from the love of God nor from God's presence with him!

Sleep finally overtook him despite the mosquitoes. He woke up early Sunday morning with the noise of the cook getting breakfast ready. He was itching all over and began to scratch the welts on his arms, neck, and forehead where the mosquitoes had feasted during the night.

About half an hour later, the cook and guard on duty began to call out, "Wake up! It's 4:30!" All the guards crawled out of bed and went over to the kitchen to hot coffee and breakfast.

Paul noticed the cook fixing another plate of food. Sure enough it was for him — more rice and a large sweet *arepa*! He tried to break off a piece of the *arepa*. Again grease oozed all around his thumb. He did not get too far with breakfast, but somehow God used his repulsion for food to begin dealing with his attitude. He realized that God had a work to do in his heart concerning this whole kidnapping and hijacking. Paul saw that he was not resting in Him.

As he pondered this, the commander walked into camp.

"How goes it?" he greeted Paul, not waiting for a response. He kept right on walking over to the radio shack. The guards had finished breakfast and filed out of camp to watch the airstrip, leaving two to guard their captive. Paul could not help but overhear the commander at the radio.

"We've got the man you're wanting," he hollered, "and the exact plane we need."

"How did you do it?" came the voice on the other end.

"Oh, we're just a good shot, that's all," the commander returned.

"OK, I want maximum security, hear?"

"Don't worry. He won't get away," the commander assured his superior.

The effect this had on Paul was anything but encouraging. He realized these were highly trained guerrillas, and they were not just playing games. Their very openness in front of him showed that they did not expect him to be able to report anything to the outside world.

The commander then took off in a speedboat and headed upriver.

Paul remained on the edge of his bunk, thinking. He quickly jotted down the day and date since he was also without a calendar now. This was Sunday, October 6. If it had not dawned on him the day before, it did now, that the guerrillas had lied to him about letting him go back to Morichal. He relived the events of Saturday, back to their landing in Morichal. And then he remembered the storm.

That storm! That's how I got here! he said almost audibly. If it hadn't been for that storm, we wouldn't have landed. We would have circled the village as usual and looked for Tim to give us the all-clear signal — but for the pressure of the storm! Now it all registered.

Then it seemed God was asking him, "Paul, who controls the weather anyway? You've been flying here in Colombia with me now for five-and-one-half years. Who controls the weather?"

"Oh Lord, You do. You control the weather!" Paul told his Father. "I remember how many times I've flown through the rain hour after hour and upon arriving at my destination You'd have it open for me to land. On longer flights where I could not have returned because of bad weather and lack of fuel, You always opened a hole in the clouds for me and gave me a way out. Oh Lord, I'm convinced that *You* control the weather!"

But God seemed to say to him, "Well then, Paul, I could just as well have had that storm right over the runway, making it impossible for you and Steve to land, right?"

"Yes, Lord, You could have," Paul acknowledged. "Then, Lord, You wanted us to land!"

It was clear now. "Then you want me *here*, Lord, right?" It began to sink in. "Well, Lord, if You want me here then I know it's for my own good, because I love You. So, Lord, I just want to thank You for bringing me here. I confess I was just not resting in You. Thanks for Your cleansing. *Thank You Lord!*"

From then on, Paul began to feel better. The nausea and the knot in his stomach disappeared. For this, again he acknowledged, "Thank You, Lord!"

"Well, Lord, what do You want me to do here?" he asked. Paul's thoughts turned from himself to the two guards who stayed with him during the day. Perhaps God wanted him to be a missionary to them. He tried to talk with them a bit. But they turned him off, as though they had orders not to become too friendly with him. He soon realized that each one was a kind of check for the other.

Later on, Paul managed to talk with one alone for quite some time. He began in Genesis and started explaining who God is. After a while, however, the guard said to him firmly, "Aww, there is no God!"

"He walked away from his shelter towards the forbidden path."
Arrow indicates where Paul stepped on a stick.
(Tim Cain's sketch of Paul's Prison Camp)

"What do you mean?" Paul asked.

"Yeah, there's no God. Have you ever seen God?" he said sneeringly.

"No, I haven't."

"See, I told you. If there was a God, you could see him."

"No," Paul answered, "the Bible says no one has seen God. It says God is Spirit, and you have to worship Him in spirit and in truth. You're trying to tell me there's no wind either, right?"

"What do you mean?"

"You say there's no God because you can't see him. Well then it's the same thing as telling me there's no wind. The wind comes from who knows where; but you can't see it, even though you try your hardest. And you never know where it's going. You just can't see the wind. So there is no wind, right?"

After a moment the guard said, "Ah, but you can see what the wind does!"

"Exactly! That's exactly right!" Paul told him. "And you can see what God does, too. That's why I'm convinced that God exists. He has done something in my heart that nothing else could do. He has given me eternal life, and that has been revealed to me through

His Word. Just look around you at all of these trees and living things — at the sky, sun, stars, moon, night, and day. God is, and He is real!"

The man paused as though pondering.

"Well, I have to go," he said. And he took off.

Others would listen for a while until something started to get personal. One of them put his situation into words for Paul.

"You know," he said, "we all decide what we want to do. You made your choice to be a missionary. Another decides to be a mechanic, another a carpenter, another a farmer. Well, I decided to be a guerrilla."

Paul replied, "That's right. We all decide what we want to do. But remember this: We either suffer the consequences of our decision, or else we enjoy the blessings from our decision."

The Sunday morning hours were long ones. Paul now doubted that God's purpose in having him there was to be a missionary to the guerrillas. They clearly did not want to listen. They had been thoroughly indoctrinated in Marxism and evolution. One fellow attempted to explain it to Paul.

"You know, you're just *matter*! You don't have a soul. For me to kill you would be just like chopping that log over there with an axe!"

Paul did not flinch a bit. He could see what guerrilla indoctrination had done for these guards. "That might be what you believe, but that's not what I believe nor what the Bible, the Word of God, says," he concluded.

The hardness of these young terrorists wore on Paul. So they had made their choice, and because of it, they had been brainwashed into believing that they had no soul. To whom would he turn to talk? They were willing to talk about other things but were so "turned off" on God. He was tempted to be discouraged, so he was glad to be able to turn to the Bible. He began in the epistles of Peter, half hoping to find something there to pass on to those guerrillas.

But no! God seemed to say to him, "Paul, *you* are the one who needs encouragement. *You* are the one who needs counsel."

Grateful for this idea, he began reading from 1 Peter 1:3 and applied it very personally. For example:

> *"Blessed be the God and Father of my Lord Jesus Christ, which according to his abundant mercy hath begotten me unto a lively hope by the resurrection of Jesus Christ from the dead, To an inheritance*

incorruptible, and undefiled, and that fadeth not away, reserved in heaven for me, Who am kept by the power of God through faith unto salvation ready to be revealed in the last time. Wherein I greatly rejoice, though now for a season, if need be, I am in heaviness through manifold temptations: That the trial of my faith, being much more precious than gold that perisheth, though it be tried with fire, might be found unto praise and honour and glory at the appearing of Jesus Christ: Whom having not seen, I love; in whom, though now I see him not, yet believing, I rejoice with joy unspeakable and full of glory."

"Whom having not seen...." Paul pondered that phrase. He had just told the guerrilla he had never seen God. What an encouragement that in *believing* lay his joy.

In short order, Paul began to be thrilled with what he had in Christ Jesus. He started feeling great, and beyond that, so great that he started thinking about escaping. He had the key. If only he could get to the airplane! But apart from God he knew that would be impossible.

That Sunday afternoon at perhaps 2:30, Paul had visitors. The commander in military uniform had gone upriver in the morning in a forty h.p. motorboat and had now returned. With him was a man in civilian clothes, looking as though he had just stepped out from behind a desk in a Bogotá office. He carried only an automatic pistol tucked in his belt; but he was accompanied by a guerrilla with a submachine gun, who seemed to be his bodyguard. A woman guerrilla, displaying the usual arms, came also. They had docked where the river ran close to the guerrilla camp.

Paul was surprised to observe that the guards did not salute their superiors. They eagerly went forward to shake their hands, however, as part of the so-called camaraderie. Then, the man in the civilian clothes began politely to set Paul "at ease" for an interrogation.

"My name is Philip," he said, "and this is my secretary, Alice. That man over there is Commander Steven" (motioning to one who had come with him). He did not introduce his bodyguard. "And *this* commander..." (turning to the one who had escorted Paul there in the plane the day before) "what name did you give him?"

"I didn't give him any name! There's no reason to tell him what my name is!"

Paul caught the fake in it all. Nevertheless, he used the names he was given.

Philip was clearly the boss. He started interrogating Paul who as yet had not been searched.

"Do you have a passport?"

"Yes, sir, but I don't carry it with me," Paul answered. "I just carry my *cedula* since I'm a resident in the country."

"May I see it?"

Paul pulled out his alien registration card and thanked God that he had rid himself of papers that should not be shown, like the address book, his car and motorcycle ownership titles. These other legal documents could be replaced, he reasoned.

At first, Paul handed him only the card he asked for, not the whole wallet. Secretary "Alice" copied carefully his name and birthdate.

"Let me see the wallet," the boss said. Paul gave it to him. This was the search he had anticipated.

The boss exclaimed, "This is really full of documents! Wow — all three: pilot's, mechanic's, and driver's licenses, both U.S. and Colombian!" He paid little attention to other papers in the wallet. From there, he asked to see what Paul carried in his pockets, bag and leather folder. The others helped in the search. "Steven" asked to see Paul's watch. He looked it over carefully, as though suspicious of a transmitter, and handed it back. The commander who had brought Paul in the previous day spotted a compact umbrella in the bag.

"I'd like to have this," he half questioned.

"Take it." Paul complied.

Satisfied, the man quit searching and handed over the bag. The others followed suit. The search was over, with Paul's ring of keys untouched.

"What do you all do down here in Colombia?" the boss asked. "We know that *missionary* is just a coverup for the CIA. We know that all missionaries work for the CIA, and they're just using the term *misionero*."

Paul contradicted. "You're wrong, sir. That might be what you believe and what you've heard, but it's not so. I know a lot of missionaries, and I can tell you the truth; not one of those I know works for the CIA. That would be dishonest, to say you're a missionary and work for the CIA. That would not please God. It's impossible to fill both those roles."

"Well, maybe not *all* missionaries," Philip conceded. "Now," he continued, "we know you have a work in Fusagasugá and that your main headquarters is there."

"No, sir, our main office is not in Fusa."

"What do you have there in Fusa?"

"Well, we have a Bible institute. We study the Bible and teach Latin Americans about God and the Bible."

"Oh, how nice!" the boss said, trying not to sound sarcastic. "Then where is your headquarters?"

Paul hated to give him any information he did not have to, but answered, "It's at Villavicencio."

"Oh, at Villavicencio. We know."

The man did not press for addresses but went back to his first question, "What does your Mission do? We know that your people from Lomalinda are working with the CIA." (Lomalinda was headquarters for SIL.)

"I know some people from Lomalinda, and I don't know of anyone there who works with the CIA."

"You mean you're not from Lomalinda? What are you?"

"I am with New Tribes Mission."

"Yes, I know. But you work with Lomalinda though."

Paul said, "No. Sometimes we have some interaction with them, but we are two completely different organizations."

"Where do you work in the tribal areas among the Indians? You work among Indians like they do, don't you?"

"Yes, we have a work with the Piapocos in Barranco Minas, with the Guayaberos in Caño Jabón, and with the Puinaves in Morichal." Paul deliberately named places the guerrillas knew and where they had already interrupted the work.

"We know where you work. You have a work with the Guananos, don't you?"

"Yes, we worked with the Guananos."

"Do you know what group we are?"

"You are the F.A.R.C.," Paul replied confidently.

"Who told you that?"

"The commander that brought me here," Paul said, motioning to the commander sitting nearby. The boss turned to him now.

"Did you tell him that?" His voice was not the least ruffled. It seemed easy for them to make up stories on the spur of the moment.

"Well, you know there are a lot of guerrilla groups, and we sort of work together. We little ones want to be part of the big group, so we say that we are from the F.A.R.C. But we belong to the E.L.P. (Ejército Liberación Popular)."

Paul did not believe him, even though no one contradicted. Both the head guerrilla at the Morichal airstrip and this commander whom they picked up on the way had plainly told him they were with the F.A.R.C. Their belt buckles said "F.A.R.C.," and they also had the F.A.R.C. "UP" insignia (Union Patriotica) on their T-shirts, standing for the political voice of the F.A.R.C. But the F.A.R.C. one-year treaty with the government was still in effect. This kidnapping would be a breach of that treaty. No wonder the boss wanted to give the lie to their identity.

"Now that I've asked you a lot of questions," the boss changed the subject, "do you have any questions to ask us?"

Paul spoke up. "I do have two questions. First, what are you going to do with me?"

"With you? You're going to be here a long, long time. We're just going to talk and get to know each other. You'll get to like it here." At that he looked over at Paul's bunk and noticed that there was neither a mattress nor a blanket. "Hey you!" he called to a guard. "Bring him a mattress and a blanket," he ordered.

The guard hustled around and brought both items. Now Paul would be able to defend himself from the mosquitoes.

The boss turned back to Paul.

"I'll be coming down now and then to visit you and will be asking you more questions which you will answer when we need to know."

Paul tried to ignore the implications of that one. "Then my next question is, 'What are you going to do with the plane?'"

The boss smiled knowingly at the other men.

"The airplane? That's really going to help us a lot. That's going to be for our service," he said.

Then Steven, the other commander, asked, "Who does the maintenance on that plane?"

Paul was uncomfortable for a second or two, but they had already seen his American and Colombian mechanic's licenses.

"I do," he answered.

All of them smiled. Those smiles said, "Aha! We have a mechanic, too!"

5

How Big Is God?

Paul's Sunday afternoon company was on the verge of leaving when one of them said, "Let's go look at the airplane!" And Paul was left alone with his thoughts.

"Lord, that plane belongs to You!" He talked it over with his heavenly Father.

The interrogation about the Mission and the plane had been so tiring. Paul had tried to explain to Philip (the guerrilla boss in the civilian clothes) what the Mission's express purpose was in being in Colombia. He explained how the missionaries had to learn the tribal language in order to teach the people about God — how He reveals Himself through the Bible. He told how they wanted the Indians to be self-sufficient and go on in God's Word by themselves, not being dependent on the missionaries. This did not score a point with Philip.

"In what other ways do you help them besides religion?" the boss had asked.

"Where we can help them with medicine, we do. In fact, just the other day, I flew a sick woman out to Mitu." Paul cited other ways in which they helped, such as literacy and agriculture, at times even purchasing needed items at cost for Indians who would send money with him — items that were not available in the jungle.

The boss had acted quite impressed. But would this prove anything before Marxist terrorists or help gain his freedom? Paul could see it would not.

Soon the group returned from the plane, talking and smiling. "We've got a real jewel there!" they were saying in effect, clearly demonstrating how pleased they were with their prize catch.

"How many planes do you have?" Philip asked.

"One," Paul answered.

"One! You have several blue and white planes too!"

Paul could see the boss still thought of him as from Lomalinda. "We only have one," he repeated. "We couldn't even afford to buy a new one. We got that one as a wreck and rebuilt it. It's like new."

This only served to impress the boss further. His captive would be an ace mechanic for *anything* that went wrong! Paul's liberty was the farthest thing from his mind. His parting words to Paul were, "We'll be seeing a lot of each other." And he took off with his companions.

Paul never saw him again.

Left alone once more, Paul sat on his bunk keeping the matter of the plane before God. "Lord, what are we (You and I) going to do?"

He wanted to believe that Tim and Bunny and Steve were freed because the plane was captured. But how could Steve get supplies out to the tribal missionaries without the plane? And if they were in the same predicament as he was....

"Lord, what are *You* going to do? These guerrillas are claiming that plane!"

This would be a hard one to turn over into God's hands. But Paul stayed with it until he could accept God's peace.

Then it was as though God said to him, "Paul, that airplane is just a hunk of metal. If I want that airplane out of here, I can get it out or I can get another one — whatever."

"OK, Lord, I'm just offering my services," Paul affirmed almost audibly. "Whatever you want! The plane is yours." A difficult surrender to make! Once made, however, Paul felt greatly relieved.

From the talk that went on around him, whether by radio or among the guards, Paul saw that they were going to do everything in their power to keep him right there. They talked openly, quite confident that he would never be free to divulge information which they would not normally want him to hear.

Guerrilla life was as busy on Sunday as on Saturday. Boats were going past Paul's camping grounds day and night — speedboats and dugout canoes — up and down the river: guerrillas, cocaine-growers, Indians, and any who were at peace with the guerrillas. Paul was surprised at the tremendously organized activity and the elaborate communication network. But he refused to be dismayed by it.

Again the Bible seemed to flip open at I Peter. In his applying I Peter personally, he paused long on the last verse of the fourth chapter.

"...let them that suffer according to the will of God..." (Yes, Lord, I know that any suffering I go through here is because it's Your will for me to be here. Thank you so much for this fact!) *"...commit the keeping of their souls to him in well doing, as unto a faithful Creator."*

Man! Paul meditated, that means I commit my soul to the One who made all creation — the moon and stars and the universe. To think of Him as a "faithful Creator" through all the history of His great power...that I can just commit my life into His hands! Sure, Paul had believed it before, but it never meant as much to him as it did now. Over and over he was finding God's grace sufficient. Now he sensed that it was God's special grace to impress this truth on him in such depth. He could see how men could have grace to be burned at the stake for Christ's sake. How it fortified him now in his own situation!

One thing more he could not pass up: he was to let God keep his soul *"in well doing, as unto a faithful Creator."* This means I am to conduct myself in submissive obedience to God the faithful Creator. The thought thrilled him — to know that the faithful Creator had him in His hands! "And You're doing a good job of it, Lord!" Paul meant it deeply.

That night he slept better in spite of the light flashing on him every three to five minutes. One guard, though, was especially annoying. He seemed to tick like a clock when it was his turn. He would walk by Paul's little abode and shine his light to see if he was still there, then back around and behind to flash it on him again.

And Sunday turned into Monday.

The same guard who was faithful at shining his big flashlight was faithful at bringing breakfast like clockwork. Paul thanked him sincerely. (Even *arepas* went down better!) He showed appreciation for every service rendered to him. He even thanked them for the humiliating times when he had to go to the woods under their armed surveillance.

This morning when Paul asked to take a bath, an idea struck him. He had missed having a towel when he took a bath, and he thought of the handy towel he had carried with him on the plane.

"Say, could I go to the airplane and get my towel?" he asked his guard.

"No way!" the guard spoke with finality. "The boss locked the doors and took the keys with him back upriver."

Paul had to keep to himself his little secret about the key in his shoe lining, which meant he would forego the luxury of the towel he might so easily have had.

Paul had another favor to ask that morning. He chose a time when the cook was preoccupied. He wanted the guard to exchange one of his gasoline barrels for another since it was cracked and leaking a gas odor that made him sick. The guard was glad to get a different one for him. But Paul had another motive in asking the favor: he wanted to retrieve some hidden documents.

While the guerrilla was over by the river, tussling with another barrel for him, Paul turned over the drum that contained a few of his documents. As water poured out through the bunghole, he was able to pull the documents on through also. Three of these were laminated and in good shape. Quickly he slipped them into his pocket, feeling he would not be searched again. The other items were mush already, so he slipped them back into the barrel and was ready to help the guard put the bed in order again.

By now, these guards seemed to want to talk with Paul, especially when they were alone in the daytime. They tried hard to get across their communist doctrines, but Paul could not keep from referring to God's Word.

"There you go again with the Bible!" one said.

"That's right. That's where I found peace with God. That's where everyone can find peace with God," Paul explained. "You know, you're trying to win peace through force — by kidnappings and threats. But you'll never get peace that way. It's only through God, through what He offers and what He plans for your life, if you will only accept it."

"Well, we've got to get going!" the guard ended the conversation.

The more Paul overheard the guards talking among themselves, the more he could see he was a "dead duck." For sure, they did not always tell the truth, even among themselves. But things they said about anyone landing on their airstrip and their references to his sleeping quarters ("That is where we put all the ones that come here.") made him see he had signed away his "bill of rights."

He was glad he had no fear of death. "Lord, I'm ready to die," he said. But he was bothered a bit by the prolonging of it: just stuck on those boards for months, eating saltless sweet *arepas* day after day! At least he realized that those who *had* had his spot before were no longer here. "There must be an end to it sometime!" he figured.

Then a new thought struck him. They would be asking for a ransom even though he doubted that they would let him out alive. Probably they would ask a large amount to include the plane also. But there was real satisfaction in the knowledge that the Mission would not pay ransom. He would rather die than be set free by ransom!

Suddenly a fear crept into his thoughts. His mind turned to loved ones outside the Mission and brothers in Christ. What if *they* decided to pay the ransom for him?

With that thought, Paul went to prayer again, "Lord, don't let them or anyone else pay!" He knew that if ransom were paid, no missionary would be safe, even in the cities. Inevitably the guerrillas would go after another, then another until soon all would have to leave without seeing their goal accomplished — that of reaching the tribal people with the Gospel of Jesus Christ.

Paul pondered it further, "It's not like a business that you can just pick up and leave. There are people living right here in this country who need to hear of God's love! The Mission needs to be able to stay here! So Lord, don't let anybody pay ransom!"

Facing imminent death, as he thought, he was assured that *"...to be absent from the body, is...to be present with the Lord"* (II Corinthians 5:8). The cause of Christ was a thousand times worth dying for. Then he began to make some comparisons: Three times in the past he had had an arrow drawn on him, and once he had been shot with a poisonous Macú dart. But those times were different, he reasoned. I would have been dying for the Lord and not for some other cause like communism. This bothered him.

"Lord," he said, "don't let me die for some stupid political cause. I want to die for You and for no other reason." No sooner had he voiced the petition than he recalled that God *wanted* him in that very place. That made a difference.

"Oh! OK, Lord. If I get killed here, it will be for You!"

Then some mundane thoughts came to the fore: Boy, I'll never eat any more ice cream (The heat intensified the desire.), and I won't ever get to use my new tools! (Bill Post, mechanic as well as pilot, had made some special tools for Paul's workshop.) Next came the dearer desires: I'll never see my daughter Lisa (who was in missionary training), nor my boys, Larry and Luke, nor Pat, my sweet wife, again. All of his loved ones and friends plus the outside world seemed so far away, just as though he were sitting on another planet.

At this point, a verse came to mind which he thought was especially apropos: *"Except a corn of wheat fall into the ground and die, it abideth alone..."* (John 12:24).

Paul saw that he had not yet "died" to self. "Lord, I don't want to abide alone!" He found it revealing, how he was clinging to things that had no eternal value — things like ice cream, tools, and what he thought were his own rights.

Immediately, he committed his family to God, knowing he would see them again one day in His presence. And as for the other things — material things that he was fond of — suddenly Paul saw that they really did not count any more. He would rather do without them than to "abide alone," unfruitful for God. He chose instead to be completely submissive to God and His perfect will. He could think of no greater joy or blessing than to have the privilege of seeing God lifted up and honored through him.

"O Lord," he prayed, "if You would be more honored and glorified through my death here, then that is what I want. But if you would get more glory by getting me out of here alive, then that is OK too, Lord. I want what You want." He paused long, being doubly sure that he meant it. Then, "Thank you, Lord."

Paul continued with his Bible reading. He encouraged himself in verses that brought out God's grace and God's mighty power. He reviewed how God always fought for his people and delivered them from their enemies when they turned to Him for help. On many occasions, they did not even have to fight; they just went out and picked up the spoil. The battle had been won already.

To bring it into the present, he reminded himself that Jesus Christ was "the same yesterday, today, and forever."

Paul put it all together. I'm going to get out of here tonight! Now that he considered himself as good as dead, he saw he had nothing to lose. He felt more confident than ever that God could do it. The plane key was a way out, yes; but the key without God involved was useless.

By slow degrees, he worked at getting a piece of log under his bed, thinking it would help make a good dummy for him when he left. He would try to get out that very night — his third night with the guerrillas. Then he wondered, And what if they catch me trying to sneak out of the camp? They'd probably either kill me or tie me to these boards.

God seemed to encourage him, "If they tie you to the boards, my grace would still be sufficient."

Hey, that's right! Paul saw it. And it gave him faith to trust God for more.

That night he did not sleep a wink. He kept waiting for the chance to sneak out of the camp and get to the airplane. He had it all planned. Only what was in his pockets would he carry out with him. He would fix the little log up in his bed along with his other belongings and make it look like his body. Then he would cover it all up with the blanket.

The guard interrupted those thoughts, shining his light, then was gone again. Later on in the night, Paul could hear a motorboat coming from downriver. When it got close, it sounded as though it was going to stop at their "port" (as they called their path to the water) at the upper end of camp. The guard, who at that time had his light on Paul, turned away and headed off to the port.

Paul came alive. Now is my chance! Quickly he grabbed the log and put it under his blanket, pushing it down to the foot of the bed.

Still in lying position, he got out from under the blanket, put on his shoes, and was arranging the blanket over his other belongings when...with a swish the guard's light swung around and stopped on Paul's net. The guard must have seen some movement in the net; so keeping the light on Paul, he came over close and shone the light right on him.

Oh, no! He caught me! Fear gripped him. The guard would have noticed that he was out from under the blanket...his shoes on...and in a most awkward position for sleeping. This was not the way the guard had just seen him when he left for the port. But Paul just lay there as stiff as a board, pretending he was asleep.

The guard kept the light on his prisoner for a while, then went over and woke up the guard who was to come on duty next. Paul could hear them talking quietly. Soon the new guard came over and shone his flashlight on Paul for quite some time. No doubt he was waiting to see if he would move from that weird position. But the only thing moving was Paul's heart thumping a prayer to God.

"O Lord, take control; *You* take control!"

The guard then went back to the first one. Could they be talking about tying him up? Soon the first guard retired to his bunk, and the guard on duty went about his normal routine. Paul gave a sigh of thanks to God. The next thing he knew, the 4 a.m. noises in the kitchen told him that Tuesday had begun.

Paul was exhausted. He had not slept for "keeping tab" on the guards that night! Surely, he had had his maximum security so far. In the morning one of the guards deliberately removed the little log Paul had put back under the bed. He felt defeated, telling himself he hadn't really trusted God to do what he knew He *could* do. Then God seemed to ask him, "Paul, what was it that encouraged you so much yesterday?"

"Your Word," Paul said, in silent prayer.

"Well...?"

Paul knew what to do. The more he read the Word, the more fortified he was.

Then a whole panorama of miracles seemed to pass before him. He was reminded of how God took the Israelites out of the land of Egypt into the promised land. How strong and powerful God had shown Himself to them in countless ways — causing plagues on their captors, changing the hearts of the Egyptians, giving the cloud to lead them by day and that pillar of fire by night! He opened the Red Sea for them to cross over on dry land; He gave them water out of a rock; He fed them with bread and meat from heaven. He even forgave their sins when they sacrificed the offerings He required. He saved them from their enemies when they turned to Him. Constantly He was making Himself real to His people.

"Lord, You are just the same yesterday, today and forever." It helped him to say so. He thought of the army that God had caused to go blind when they went to seize Elisha (II Kings 6) and of Saul's men out after David, when God caused a deep sleep to fall on the whole army (I Samuel 26). He said, "God, I know You can do the same thing with these few guerrillas. You can make them fall into a deep sleep, and You can cause them not to see when I leave!"

God seemed to answer him, "Well, Paul, if you know I can do that, why don't you trust me with it?"

"OK, Lord."

All this, Paul applied to the present. It thrilled him that this same God was living in his heart because he trusted in the sacrifice

Paul and Pat Dye with Luke, Lisa, and Larry

of His Son Jesus Christ. To think that he too had a right, as God's child, to expect to see God do the impossible! Yet, if he were to be killed, that same power of God that raised Jesus from the dead would raise him also at Christ's return.

By this time Paul was thoroughly excited at the limitless power of God. He was convinced that this night, Tuesday, the 8th of October, was the night.

In the meantime, back at the Mission home, God was upholding Paul's wife, Pat, as He was the others involved. She was amazed at her own fortitude on learning that the guerrillas must have taken Paul off with the plane. Then she learned from one person after another how many were praying, both during the day and at night. Mary Cain helped her put a call through to her mother in Chicago, and in turn her mother alerted many other groups and individuals to pray.

Two older ladies on the school staff at the *finca* were specially faithful in prayer when others were asleep. One of them, known to the children as "Grandma Poulsen," assured Pat, in her English accent, "Mark my words, Pat, God will answer our prayers and bring Paul back very soon, and he'll be telling his story with tears in his eyes." Pat knew Grandma Poulsen as a woman who walked with God and could not lightly dismiss her words.

Work had to continue, nevertheless, and Pat had many occasions to meet with folks outside the Mission. First there were four men who had been putting gravel on the public road which passed through the Mission property. They needed a meal. As Pat fed them, they could not help but make reference to the impossible situation her husband was in. Lamely they told Pat her husband would be all right, each in his own way. This gave her a chance to witness of her all-powerful God.

Concerned neighbors told Pat how they had had dreams in which Paul came out all right. But she put no stock in dreams. Their coming, however, was Pat's opportunity to show how the peace of God ruled in her heart.

One of the neighbors, seeing that Pat did not cry nor live in constant anguish, questioned whether Pat really loved Paul. Pat soon dispelled that notion! All that worried her was why God kept some older and younger people in the Mission praying during the night, while she herself slept like a baby. She could only wait on Him and lean the harder.

Throughout Sunday, Pat had more time to think of the consequences of Paul's captivity. Like others of the Mission, she knew it was a matter of death or an absolute miracle. Throughout their married life she had often faced the possibility of not having her husband return: from trips on contact work in Venezuela, from plane trips in Panama, from many visits to supply the missionaries who were with the wild Macú, and in recent years, from the constant dangers of guerrilla ambush in the tribal areas. Even cocaine-growers were a menace to planes flying low over their fields.

Pat's mind turned to the first imminent death threat Paul had had in the jungles of Venezuela — traumatic for her because it happened on their fourth anniversary:

> Paul and another young missionary were seeking a friendly contact with a new Yanomamö group up in the grasslands of Indian territory. Four professing Christian Yanomamö accompanied them. In a jungle village on the way to the grasslands, one of the four Indians, named Chiverito, overheard a plot to kill all six of the travelers in order to take their possessions — coveted machetes, flashlights, and guns especially. Chiverito was shaken.
>
> Very quietly, he said to Paul, "Give me a paper and pencil." He wrote what he had heard — a well-formed plan — not daring to

speak of it aloud. Then he turned to Paul's missionary companion and said, "I need a gun and five shells to go hunting." Strange as the request seemed so late in the day, the missionary would not shame him in front of strangers and granted his request. Chiverito picked up the gun and five shells with his flashlight and disappeared down the path. Everyone wondered what he was up to.

Paul set up his crude radio that night and called to Pat. Just as Pat was expecting a "Happy Anniversary, Sweetheart!" she got Paul's SOS: "Tell everyone on the field to pray for us. They plan to kill all six of us. And pray for Chiverito who hasn't returned from hunting. If we're still here in the morning, I'll call you."

God heard prayer that night. The enemy host — in that round-house of many families — kept waiting till all six were together. "Has he come back yet? Has he come back yet?" they called out through the night. But Chiverito never returned.

Next morning, when the other five resumed their journey with two new guides (who had opposed the plot to kill the six), they found Chiverito down the path glad to see them alive and anxious to continue the trip. He quickly explained to Paul why he had left. "I saw no way we could be saved," he said, "so I took the five shells to be ready to revenge your five deaths first when they came to kill me!" — a noble Yanomamö sign of love!

Paul was horrified and explained to his young friend that "God is the One who can revenge us. He is powerful enough to take care of us at any time. And you see He did!"

Paul called Pat that morning, and they praised God together.

Now as evening wore on that Sunday night, a verse was coursing through her mind: *"...I will never leave thee, nor forsake thee. So that we may boldly say, The Lord is my helper, and I will not fear what man shall do unto me"* (Hebrews 13:5,6).

Pat relaxed at the thought and dwelt on it. It fortified her to continue to trust in the One who promised to be her helper, no matter what man might do. Then she went on to the first six verses of James. She thanked God for the exhortations she found. But there in the margin of her Bible she saw some familiar handwriting. She had never known Paul to write in *her* Bible, but he had written by those verses, "Hold up courageously under fire. ENDURANCE!"

Pat shared this special message with her youngest son, Luke. Then followed what seemed like an hour of discussion with his inquisitive mind, and both went to bed for the night.

The following day, Pat was feeling a little less stoic when she had to wash Paul's laundry. Thinking that she might never see him again, his very shirts seemed almost sacred to her. She took one of his shirts, with the dirt and smell still fresh within it, and put it away in a plastic bag.

Silly! she said to herself. The separation must be having its effect on me. But I'll just keep it there till I have him back in my arms!

6

Mid Friends and Enemies

Down in Morichal, with no place to go, Steve thought of the times he had wished he could get away from his busy schedule to spend more time with God — off to some desert place. Now he realized he had found that place! He had all the time he wanted for reading the Word and praying, either by himself or together with the Cains. This, of course, was not exactly what he had had in mind!

Steve had known the Cains somewhat but never in such close fellowship as they were having now. The very terms of their "arrest" provided a closeness. What came to the fore was their oneness in Christ. Steve had shared with Tim and Bunny the verses that came to him along the path from the airstrip. The Cains, too, shared verses that were meaning a lot to them. Tim had abandoned his first feelings that God had "betrayed" him. He found it uplifting to realize that God was as much in control of things now as He was when all went well.

As the three missionaries feasted on different portions of the Bible, God dealt with their hearts. They did not like some things they found in their inmost being — clinging to *things* and *rights* which they unconsciously thought they deserved. No doubt theirs were some of the same discoveries Paul was making in his confines. This trio in Morichal found no hesitation in confessing things to each other. Then they prayed, alone and together. It seemed they were learning as a unit, being refined and brought to greater spiritual maturity. The three had no way of knowing that many were praying that they would be allowed to be together — ever since word got around that the plane was gone and that Steve was still in Morichal.

One passage stood out as very personally theirs:

> *"...for we have no might against this great company that cometh against us; neither know we what to do: but our eyes are upon thee."*
>
> *"...Be not afraid nor dismayed by reason of this great multitude; for the battle is not yours, but God's"* (II Chronicles 20:12,15).

The Bible expressed it so much better than they could — the helplessness they felt, yet the knowledge that nothing was too hard for God.

Tim thanked God that his parents would look out for their two girls if he were killed. Then he added, "But Lord, You gave them to *me* and I ought to take care of my responsibility, You know!"

Psalm 91 was a special encouragement in the direction of deliverance:

> *"He that dwelleth in the secret place of the most High shall abide under the shadow of the Almighty. I will say of the LORD, He is my refuge and my fortress; my God; in him will I trust. Surely he shall deliver thee from the snare of the fowler, and from the noisome pestilence."*

They talked more than once of the possibility of escaping. But one thing they all agreed on: it would be all three of them or none!

The rest of Psalm 91 seemed to apply to their situation also:

> *"He shall cover thee with his feathers, and under his wings shalt thou trust; his truth shall be thy shield and buckler. Thou shalt not be afraid for the terror by night; nor for the arrow that flieth by day; Nor for the pestilence that walketh in darkness..."*

"Man!" said Steve, the first time he noticed the last sentence, "That means our guards — *'the pestilence that walketh in darkness'!* They make so much noise at night, keeping us awake, shining their lights right in our eyes." The noisiest of the guards they had dubbed "Music Box," since no guard would give his own name. He played his own wild music on Tim's little cassette player as he walked around on guard duty.

Tim had a ukulele that helped the three captives keep in tune when they sang together. The song that meant the most to them — which they later called their theme song — was a part of Psalm 25:

> *"Unto thee, O LORD, do I lift up my soul. O my God, I trust in thee: let me not be ashamed, let not mine enemies triumph over me.*
>
> "Yea, let none that wait on thee be ashamed: let them be ashamed which transgress without cause.
>
> *"Shew me thy ways, O LORD; teach me thy paths. Lead me in thy truth, and teach me: for thou art the God of my salvation; on thee do I wait all the day."*

It took a while for Tim and Steve to learn that they could not talk with the guerrillas when two or more were present. That is, they could not talk about anything personal. Only God could give them love for these guards; and God did. They watched for any chance to befriend them for His sake.

"Tell us about your family," they said to one.

"Oh, we're not allowed to talk about that," was the answer.

The missionaries saw those young terrorists as being in pitiable bondage. From elsewhere, Tim had been informed of promises made to teenagers who were invited to join the guerrillas: "good salary with vacations and all for a good cause." But the young people discovered it was rough living and very lonely. Friends and relatives complained that their loved ones were sent so very far away. Vacations would not be forthcoming for years. The few times they were allowed to go to town, they were not permitted to be alone even for conversations with a friend or relative. And if one escaped, he was tracked down until he was found and not allowed to live. He "knew too much," or he "talked too much," as far as the guerrilla superiors were concerned.

One night, a guard sat down at the table where Tim and Steve were talking. He had become quite relaxed with these missionaries who never gave him any trouble. Tim and Steve asked him some questions about religious liberty in Russia and Cuba since he assumed a relationship with the communists of those countries.

"Is it true they have evangelical churches in Cuba?"

"Oh, yes, the communists have nothing against religion."

"Are there churches in Russia?"

"Oh, yes, I'm sure there are. We're not against religion," he emphasized.

"Then why are we held captive because we are doing religious work?" Tim asked.

"I don't know," he hedged. He had not thought of that one. "There are some things they don't tell us."

The guard had set his gun down on the table and yawned. Then his head fell lower and lower down on his arms to the table, and soon he was fast asleep.

Tim and Steve looked at each other and grinned, pointing to the gun which either one could easily have picked up. The guard had already bragged that it could shoot a hole through the steel of a railway track or shoot down an airplane.

Tim, not wanting the guard to be caught napping, gave him a hard nudge on the arm. "Hey! You'd better go make your rounds of the house!" he said, "or you'll get in trouble."

The guard woke up, startled, not seeming to know where he was for an instant. Then he shook himself and went back on duty.

The Puinaves continued to come by on any pretext just to check on the missionaries. Sometimes they were permitted to come in the house, a few at a time, but always within earshot of the guards. Those who were outside often spoke boldly to the other guerrillas. Tim kept his ear cocked for those conversations. He heard Alberto, the village leader ask one of them, "Why do you have these people? They haven't done anything!"

"Well, we're investigating. We think they're evil people."

"I can guarantee you they're not!" Alberto affirmed. "These people have been with us for over three years now, and they've done nothing but good to us. They've taught us the Word of God, they've helped us when we were sick, and they haven't charged for the medicine. They've brought things back from town for us. If you want to catch somebody evil, there are all kinds of evil guys running around.

"Look at all those drug workers," Alberto continued. "They come through here and sell us a pair of batteries for a super high price. They charge us so much for these little things we need — soap, salt, fishhooks — that we can't pay for them. Timoteo hasn't done that!" On and on he went, trying to persuade the guerrillas to release the missionaries.

In the evenings, the guerrillas met with the Puinaves over at the community house. Often Tim could overhear what was being said. The guerrillas tried to convince the Puinaves that the missionaries were bad.

"No," contradicted the Puinaves, "they are *not* bad!"

Then the guerrilla up in front told how terrible all Americans were, listing wartime matters as regular atrocities...beginning at Hiroshima. "These missionaries are CIA agents," he added. "They are organizing massacres of women and children. Americans," he continued, "are in cahoots with the Colombian government to take all the natural resources away from the poor people."

"No, no, no! That's not true! These people are *not* like that! You're wrong! That's not right!" For many of the Indians, however, the Spanish went right over their heads.

"Well, these Americans treat you nice because they're trying to get something out of you. It won't be long till they'll do something really terrible to you. You can't pet a tiger!"

One of the Puinaves, characteristically quiet but seething inside, sat back saying inaudibly to the guerrilla, "*You* are the tiger!"

Though the guerrilla brainwashing session kept the believers from their nightly Bible study in the church, Alberto saw to it that they met later and had their own service. The believers shared one big prayer request — the cry of each of their hearts — that God would stop the guerrillas from bothering their beloved Tim and Bunny.

The guerrillas called the Puinaves Tim's "family." They were amazed at how these Indians loved the Cains. Guerrilla tactics had always been to try to win the Indians' confidence from the first — to keep telling them that only they, the guerrillas, sought their good, that the government did not. And they added, "Is there any Colombian bothering you? If so, you tell *us* and we'll take care of him."

Tim knew they would follow through in such a case. From the Indians, he had learned so much of how the guerrillas functioned. It always amazed him how these Indians knew facts of which people in the cities were not aware. Their grapevine along the rivers was very effective, even from tribe to tribe.

There had been the time when a cocaine-grower felt his work was thwarted when missionaries told some Christian Indians that it was against the law for them to farm cocaine. That man aimed his hatred at two missionaries in different locations of a non-Puinave tribe. The Indians discovered that the man went to the guerrillas (to whom he regularly paid "taxes") and asked them to do away with those missionaries. Immediately the Indians approached the cocaine-grower threateningly.

"You'd better get out of here if you know what's good for you!" they said.

The man believed them. He picked up his valuables and hot-footed it out of the area.

However, woe to any group of Indians who got in the way of the guerrillas! When the friendship tactics did not work, they tried instilling fear. This might mean killing two or three of them in order to produce fear of disobedience in the rest.

Near the beginning of the Cains' captivity, Tim thought he needed to clarify something with the guerrillas. He spoke to the guards who were then in the house.

"If you guys are thinking of ransom money, I can tell you now that you are not going to get it. It is not our Mission policy to pay ransom. In fact, we have all signed a paper saying that we agree with our Mission policy that they will not pay ransom or comply with any other demands that captors may ask."

One of the guerrillas seemed quite concerned about Tim's announcement. He ran out of the house and spoke to the other guerrillas excitedly.

"Did you hear what he said?" And he continued more quietly to pass on Tim's words. He seemed worried for quite a while. Doubtless he had counsel over the jungle camp radio later on. The next day, he came back.

"When we took you it wasn't for ransom. It had to do with some investigation." The missionaries never knew how much to believe of what the guerrillas said. In fact, their guards told so many obvious lies that the trio doubted almost everything. They learned to take anything that was said "with a grain of salt." Further, it was clear that the guards themselves did not know all that was going on behind the scenes.

One day Tim talked with the youngest of the group, whom the trio had dubbed "the Kid."

"Why did you come from so far away and sacrifice so much just to teach the Bible?" the Kid asked, after some conversation.

"Have you ever read the Bible?" Tim asked. "Or do you know anything about it?"

"No, we don't believe in the Bible. We guerrillas are taught scientifically so we don't have to *believe*. We can *know* the truth." Then he went on to give Tim a simple explanation of the theory of evolution.

"I have a problem with evolution," Tim responded. "It's harder for me to believe in evolution than in what the Bible says, because that theory states that everything just started by itself. Where did that *everything* come from? I can explain it the way the Bible says because God did it. He was always there, and He is all powerful and very wise, and He is the one that started the whole thing."

The young guerrilla did not know what to say.

Tim pressed a bit. "What do you guys say about how things got started?"

"Well, it's very scientific, and they haven't explained it all to us yet."

"Well, I'd check into it if I were you. And if you can convince me that what you have is true, I'll believe it. I'm not just taking the Bible because someone *told* me it's true. It's real in my life. I know that God speaks to me every day through His Word."

The Kid had no answer for that one. He dropped the subject.

The guerrillas seemed quite concerned about Tim's illness. Though there were definite symptoms of filaria, he broke out in red blotches also. He seemed to get worse rather than better and was in fact losing weight for lack of appetite.

One of the guerrillas had an answer. "I have some intravenous injections here for stomach trouble," he said. "Let me give you one."

"No, no," Tim pleaded. "It's not my stomach that's ailing."

For a time it seemed the guard would win out, and Tim was "scared to death." But somehow the guerrilla was persuaded not to administer the injection. By slow degrees, Tim began to get better.

Bunny was normally on a hypoglycemia diet; but nothing bothered her now except a hyperacidity in her stomach which was very uncomfortable. It had begun with the appearance of the first guerrilla, and she sensed a need to calm down inside. She prayed for relief, but it did not come immediately.

About the sixth day of captivity, Tim asked if he could talk with Alberto who was working on a canoe just behind the house.

"Sure," they said. "Go ahead!"

Tim stepped outside the house and was glad he could talk alone with this Puinave believer. He reassured him that the three were fine, that nothing out of the way had been done to them up to that point.

Alberto had much to share about how God had helped him when his old desires came back to him. In this case, the temptation was a desire to take Tim's defense into his own hands. Revenge killing had once been an important part of his culture, and if he ever had a reason to go back to it, it was now. Others reminded him that their ancestors were fierce. They still knew how to make war clubs! "These guerrillas are bothering God's servants!" they said, to defend their intentions.

But Alberto's life had changed with the Gospel. Tim had taught them *"...Love your enemies,...do good to them that hate you"* (Matthew 5:44). Nevertheless, all night Alberto was tempted to evil thoughts. Then God "pulled them back" from him. Again, he wanted to give in to the old desires. But God "pulled them back" from him again. Alberto expressed it as though it had been a tug-of-war all night long until God won out. Finally, he left it in God's hands. He told his people next morning, "No, God does not want us to kill the guerrillas."

A visiting chief from downriver went to Alberto's house that very morning. He had the same intentions. Wouldn't that be the noble thing to do — to defend Tim from his enemies? But Alberto was able to remind him of God's Word. "God wouldn't want that," he told him. "God told me last night that we should leave it in His hands."

To Tim, he added, "If that chief had come to me one day earlier, we might have done the wrong thing!"

Tim responded, "That's right, Alberto. I want you to stand fast on the Word of God. I don't want you to do anything else! Just listen to Him!"

Tim was thrilled to know that they had listened to God's voice within them and had resisted temptation!

Tim and Bunny explained to the Puinaves also that the Mission had made a decision never to pay ransom for a missionary. So Tim told them that now they expected to be killed. Several who were standing around spoke up, offering to defend Tim and Bunny even to the point of death.

"No," said Tim, "If they kill us, that's all right. God didn't promise us we would live easy lives. On the contrary, the Bible says we will have afflictions because we are His children. It will be harder for you because there will be no one to teach you. But God, the Holy Spirit, is in your hearts to teach you. I want you to carry on yourselves and stand firmly in God's Word. You know the truth now."

The believers gave rapt attention to every word Tim had to say, as though to a dying man. Then some of them wanted to know just what the guerrillas had confiscated. Tim tried to explain. They no longer had their radio or tape recorder or many of the things they had used daily. "But I don't know what they took from the Van Allens' house," he said. "It's a wreck."

Tim, knowing that Alberto would be going downriver to meet with those who gathered for the convention, had a bright idea. He stepped inside and handed over to Alberto the fifteen gallons of gasoline that Paul had left with him before. "Better for him to have it than these guerrillas," he told himself. A guard looked on and, by silence, gave consent to whatever Tim was doing.

Chicho was standing with the group all this time. He was recalling a day when his house had burned to the ground months before. As he had looked on sadly, Tim had come alongside to comfort and help him. Tim took the family a meal, helping in every way he could, then reminded Chicho of Bible truths.

"That's all right, Chicho," Tim had said. "These are just material, temporal things. God is powerful enough to give all of these things back to you!" And Chicho had watched that very truth come to pass. First, one villager had brought him something he needed, then another and another; and God did give him back the things he lost. Besides, Chicho had seen a blessing that came from that fire. A community guest house next to his had caught fire and had burned to the ground. In it, some cocaine makers were making themselves more and more at home, to the chagrin of the village. After the fire, it was never rebuilt, and the cocaine makers took their business elsewhere.

Now Chicho spoke up regarding Tim's losses to the guerrillas, "These are just material things, Timoteo. God can give all this back to you. What we're concerned about is *you*!"

A big smile crossed Tim's face. Here was the pupil giving his teacher the truth that had meant so much to him. How it encouraged Tim to see the *life* that was there within them! It was so real, burning in their hearts, that God was able to deal with them. He took advantage to teach them further. "Do good to your enemies!" He reminded them of the verse *"...if thine enemy hunger, feed him..."* (Romans 12:20). They took it literally.

Imagine the surprise of the guerrillas when one Puinave family sent them a big bowl of cooked food. Another took some ripe bananas over to where they ate in Van Allens' kitchen. Others followed suit. These believers were "heaping coals of fire on their heads." The guards could not figure out what had happened, nor could they believe it was simply because of the power of God's Word.

Tim was greatly uplifted after talking with these Indian brothers in Christ. It did not occur to him till later that his prayer that God would "send something that would shake them up" had indeed been answered. Thinking of Alberto, Chicho, and many others for whom God's Word had become a way of life, it seemed that now he

Tim at language study with a Puinave friend

could face death. His goal somewhat fulfilled, he felt for a moment like Simeon, *"Lord, now lettest thou thy servant depart in peace..."* (Luke 2:29).

Then again he thought of his girls. They needed him and Bunny. And he thought of the teaching he still had in store for this baby church, for he was only up to Romans in his careful teaching through the whole Bible. True, they had a translation of sorts, done with the help of an Indian of another tribe for whom Puinave was a second language. A revision was being worked on. But they still needed the teaching in their own language.

"Lord, I believe you still have work for me to do." And now, more than ever since his captivity, Tim was hopeful that God would get him out of there alive.

Tim became the optimist of the three. The other two did not want to entertain false hopes that God would deliver them *physically*. Tim told them, "I *know* the Lord is going to get us out of here because I haven't finished the job."

"What about me?" asked Steve.

"Yeah, you, too, Steve — all three of us, together."

7

Thank You, Lord

On Tuesday evening, October 8, Paul was still tingling with excitement at what God could do. With just His Word as inspiration, he began afresh to plan his escape. He figured that the maximum amount of fuel he had left in the plane was about twenty gallons. This would be enough to fly almost one-and-one-half hours — not enough to get him home but enough to get him a long way from the guerrillas!

I'll have to take off in the dark, he told himself, but I surely don't want to have to land in the dark!

Paul then resolved to sleep, and he would count on leaving just before dawn. This way, it would be daylight by the time he needed to land. Without a watch, he would just trust God to give him a good sleep in spite of the flashlight check-ups and to wake him up at the right time.

That night he slept so soundly he forgot where he was, until a light in his face disturbed him. He squinted his eyes open. "Oh! the guard checking on me! Oh, yeah! *Here's* where I am."

Suddenly his tune changed.

"Oh yes! This is the night I'm going to leave! Thanks, Lord, for waking me up!"

As soon as the guard left, Paul sat up in bed. He had no knowledge of the time but figured it must be getting on toward morning. If the moon should come up right then, he knew it would be harder to trust God for a safe getaway! "Now is the time to go!" he said, "before the moon comes up and before the guard shines his light again, making his rounds."

Paul bowed his head, "Dear Lord, I ask you to blind the eyes of the guards who are awake and make their ears deaf so they can't hear. And Lord, the ones who are asleep...make them sleep so soundly that they won't wake up...Thank you, Lord." His heart pounded with excitement.

Seconds were passing quickly, and it was all very quiet — too quiet.

"I'll wait till I hear someone snoring," Paul decided, "then I'll know God is answering my prayer."

But no one snored.

He lay back down in bed again, listening and waiting.

More precious seconds were flitting by. Somehow he could not manage to get himself to lift up the side of his mosquito net to get out. And he still could not hear anyone snoring.

Just then the guard came back and shone his light on him. Fear gripped him again.

The guard turned and walked away.

In that second, Paul sensed a gentle prodding from God. He was reminded of how Israel came up against the Jordan River: Joshua told them, *"as soon as the soles of the feet of the priests...shall rest in the waters..."* that God would part the water, and all would go across on dry ground.

Paul got the point immediately. It was as though God was saying, "Paul, as soon as you get your feet out of this mosquito net, I'll do *My* part!"

"OK, Lord." Immediately he got up, and, with the mosquito net draped over his back, he began to make a dummy. He bunched up his extra set of clothes and placed them with his leather bag in position for his head and body. The leather folder with his Bible and study notes he stood on end, wide open, at the bottom for his feet. Then, in the darkness, he spread his blanket over all of it and hoped it would look like him. In a second, he came out from under the mosquito net, tucked it under the mattress, and started taking one step at a time.

Carefully and oh, so quietly he walked away from his shelter toward the forbidden path. With each step, out of his heart welled a sincere, warm "Thank you, Lord." When he got right in front of the last shelter before reaching the path that would lead him away from camp, he stepped on a branch. It broke under his weight and made a loud *Crack!*

Oh, nooo! Paul froze, expecting to have a light turned in his direction. But there was no light. No noise. Paul went on. In his heart, he underlined a "Thank you, Lord" of relief. Soon, he was on the trail and, with each step, his thank you's to the Lord came faster and faster.

In the darkness, Paul could tell that the woods and the trail were all wet. He realized anew how well he had slept since it apparently had rained during that time.

"Thank you, Lord. The leaves make a lot less noise this way," he said inwardly.

Paul walked faster and faster down the 700-meter path toward the plane. But the night was pitch black, and he soon lost the trail. He found himself tangled up in some thick bushes and vines and had to grope to find his way again to the trail. Next, he was lost on the other side of the path, climbing over logs that he knew were not on the path.

Slow down, Paul, he chided himself. When he found the path again, he walked half stooped over so that he could feel the path with his hands. In those tense moments, not a thought entered his mind about the creatures which come out at night to hunt and crawl and slither. He concentrated only on staying in the path and going forward.

Paul had learned another lesson by this time. God was just as able to help him walking carefully as rushing quickly. He was going to have to continue trusting Him to keep those guerrillas asleep, blinded and deaf until he escaped.

When Paul finally got to where he figured the plane ought to be, there was no plane to be seen. But out of the pitch blackness he thought he detected the form of a house. He had not noticed a house there before.

Man! Did I take the wrong trail? was his first thought. What if there's someone sleeping in it? He crept up to it and put out his hand to feel it. It was the airplane! It had been covered with black plastic; then logs and palm leaves had been spread out over the wings.

"Oh no!" he stood aghast. "I have to get rid of all that stuff before I can even turn the plane around!" And it was still parked facing into the trees. What an enormous job for a quick getaway! There was no way he could turn the plane once he started the motor, as there was not enough room to swing the tail in place because of the trees and poles which were so close on either side.

Paul began to wish Steve had come along. Two were needed to accomplish the task before him. Yet he recognized the wish as futile immediately. How could the two of them ever have kept up communication together — probably each in a different place in camp

— to leave unnoticed at the same time? And he knew he would never have taken off alone if he were leaving Steve behind.

Don't stand around! Get busy! he prodded himself.

Everything was wet on top and muddy below from the rain. He removed the palm, the logs, and the plastic and cleared it away, feeling blindly in the dark. Next, he wiped the whole airplane off with his outstretched arms. He found the sensor antenna was wrecked by a log hanging over it which had stretched the attaching spring badly. Then he prayed for strength to move the plane.

First, he pulled it back and forth until he slipped and wrenched his back. Not wanting to risk another slip in the mud, he took his shoes off so as to have better traction with his toes. With his shoes in his hands and wondering where to put them, he remembered the key in the lining.

"Man! I don't dare lose *that!*" he gasped. So he pulled the ignition key out of his shoe and stuck it between his teeth. Then he had second thoughts. What if I slip in this mud again and fall and lose the key? He knew he would never find it in that inky darkness. So he stuck it down deep in his watch pocket and kept right on working.

By feeling with his hands, he checked to see how far the wing tips were from the trees, then moved the plane some more, tugging and pulling. Sometimes he would have to feel in front and behind the tires to see if there were any obstacles hindering the movement of the plane. Once, it would not roll forward or backward. With a little checking he found that the tail wheel was up against a stump. Again he had to ask God for strength to lift the tail of the plane up over the stump. Finally, he had the airplane turned around and headed the right way. Altogether, Paul's struggles there with the plane had taken at least twenty minutes to half an hour.

Now for the runway! Could they have put barrels in the way — either on the 200-meter road that led to it or on the runway itself? His pilot's caution would not allow him to run the risk; and he did not dare start the motor until he was sure he was ready to go. So he felt his way out to the runway, still barefoot. He found a fifty-five-gallon drum at the entrance to the runway which he easily removed. From there, after going a few more meters, he would hazard a guess that all was clear rather than risk getting lost again in the thick darkness.

When he got back to the plane again, he was exhausted; but he could not start the motor yet. He still had to check the tanks. Now he needed the key to the door to get his dip stick. For a moment, he was confused.

Oh, my key! Where is it? Did I drop it? The scare only lasted for seconds until he remembered placing it in his watch pocket. "Thank you, Lord!" Quickly he opened the door and placed the key in the ignition switch, confident that it would not get lost in there.

Paul climbed up on the left wing with the dip stick and suddenly realized he would not be able to *see* where the gas level was. But he pulled it out and smelled from top to bottom. Not a whiff of gas! Then he found his way to the right side. This time, by smelling, he found gas two thirds of the way down the stick. "Ahaaa!" he breathed a glad sigh of relief and gratefulness.

He began to move faster. "I can't spend any more time here!" he goaded himself as he climbed up and strapped himself in. He turned around to shut the door.

Suddenly he heard three heavy footsteps: Crunch! Crunch! Crunch!

Paul, who knew well the noises of the jungle — a deer bounding, a tapir or a fox running — had no problem deciphering the sound of a man's footsteps. It came from the direction of the mouth of the path and sounded like someone stepping on the debris he had thrown down.

They're here! he thought, What'll I do? His heart sank. But no one shone a light. The last footstep was stopped in its track a few feet away. Paul had gone so far now, constantly acknowledging God's help, that he felt sure he was not to turn back. "If they want to shoot me, they'll have to shoot me," he said inaudibly. Without losing a second, he shut and locked the door.

Simultaneously, he pushed the mixture in, pulled on the master, primed the engine, and turned the key to start the motor. To his joy, it cranked up immediately. Notably, this was a noisier motor than the usual Cessna 185, so the cat was out of the bag now. He turned on the taxi light, pulling the switch farther to use the landing light. But the bulb had burned out! With just the taxi light, Paul tried to look out, only to find that he couldn't see. His heated body had caused the windows to fog up!

He opened up his side windows to see if that would help, then reached under the seat for the towel he always kept there. Happily he grabbed it and wiped at the windows — inside and out with a quick swipe. The three steps had made him move faster! If it was a guerrilla, God must have paralyzed him! True, it could have been an angel; but there was no reassurance that it was.

When the taxi light revealed the road ahead, Paul realized his towel had not accomplished too much on the windows. He could hardly see a thing. A ground fog enveloped everything, even the limbs sticking out into the road. He taxied forward carefully, fully realizing that he could be heard by the guerrillas on ahead at the other end of the airstrip. About halfway out to the strip the tires slipped sideways in the ruts and put the wings precariously close to some trees.

"Oh no!" Paul groaned, "My wing isn't going to clear those trees. I don't dare get out, and even if I did, I probably couldn't push the plane out of the ruts by myself."

"Lord, please hold this left brake!" he prayed. Then pushing full left rudder, he gave the engine a burst of power. The plane responded well and came out of the ruts as the wing tip just scraped by the trees. "Thank you, Lord."

Out at the entrance to the runway, things were worse yet. Paul couldn't see a thing for the fog. It was exceptionally thick and right down on the ground. "Lord...Why? You have brought me this far, and now I can't see to take off."

"Get going, Paul!" God seemed to say. The noisy motor would awaken the commander and others in the houses, as well as the guards at the far end of the runway — if it had not already! And it must be nearly getting-up time, he figured.

"OK, Lord," Paul responded. Setting his altimeter on zero, he pulled one notch of flaps on, then opened up the door to see if he could see any better. The taxi light reflected back in his eyes, but a lot less than it had through the windshield. He held the door open with his shoulder and continued to taxi slowly as he made a vague right turn. Next thing he saw some weeds and branches coming at him.

"Oops! That's not the strip," he directed himself, and swung to the left and continued to taxi. Then he spotted some weeds that had to be along the edge of the runway.

"There it is!" he exclaimed and continued to taxi just to be sure the edge of the strip was consistent. Reassured, he "poured on the power."

With the engine now roaring full blast for a takeoff, Paul hung out the door, keeping his light on the row of weeds with the rudder. The tires were throwing up mud and water which the prop blast was slamming into his eyes and face; but that didn't matter now! He hung out there until he was airborne, then closed the door.

Inside now, he held the heading on his directional gyro (DG). Looking at the DG and altimeter, he called off the altitude as he roared up into the air: "100 ft...200 ft...300 ft...Aaaaa...." Relief! He knew now that he was clear of the trees.

A sensation of freedom sent a thrill through his being. God had proven Himself, for sure, to be the God of the impossible. In fact, it seemed God had allowed enough obstacles to let him see it as *extra* impossible. From Paul's heart welled one deep, long thank You, Lord!

8

In the Clouds

One thought had persisted as Paul kept going straight ahead: Would any guerrillas from the houses or at the far end of the runway try to shoot at him? They could not help but hear the plane's motor when he had roared over them on takeoff. In answer to that question, he began to see the reason for the awful ground fog. They might have seen a general glow of his lights, but with that fog, any light beamed toward the little Cessna would only bounce back to them. How he thanked God for planning the rain and the ground fog — let alone the silence of the guards!

Paul had yet more hurdles to clear once he was in the air. He had no information on the barometric pressure, so he had set his altimeter on zero before takeoff. This would give him a reference to his altitude above the ground. Quickly, he reached 2,000 feet.

He tried to read his master compass but could not even see it. Normally it should have a little light in it, but he had never had occasion to use it before since night flying was illegal in the jungle.

Oh, no! he said to himself, Where am I going?

The farther he got from his captors, however, the more he thanked God for his newly found freedom. Then he did some tall thinking to get a light on that compass. He fooled with the dome light until he finally ripped it off the ceiling and turned it on to the master compass. He set his directional gyro to it, then headed north.

The left gas gauge was on Empty, and the other marked a quarter of a tank.

"Lord, I don't know how far I'm going to go, but You take me as far as You can," Paul prayed.

He continued to climb until, at 3,000 feet, he broke out of the ground fog and cloud cover which lay over the jungle floor. He turned off the taxi light only to realize there had to be another cloud layer above him. He could not see a thing in the pitch black darkness. Not a star could be seen.

For the first time since leaving camp, Paul began to wonder what time it was. His watch was still useless without batteries. But sure enough, there was the clock in the panel. It read 06:58 or 6:58 a.m.

Man! The sun should be out, he reasoned, but it's awfully dark!

Then it came back to him. Oh, yeah, that's zulu time! For local time, I take away five. That means 1:58 instead of 6:58? It can't be!

But he knew it had to be. Figuring on eight minutes' flying time already, he saw he must have taken off at 1:50 a.m. That meant (with a maximum one-and-a-half hours worth of fuel) he had to land by 3:20 a.m.

"Set this bird down somewhere while it's still night — still dark?" He struggled to get it into his head. For a few seconds, it looked impossible. But he was quickly reminded that God had just handled the impossible!

"You got me out from down there safely," he said aloud to Him. "You can get me back on the ground again safely. Thank You, Lord."

Carefully maintaining his heading, Paul looked over to the co-pilot's seat and discovered his helmet lying there.

"All right!" he said, reaching for it, and pulling it down on his head. It felt good to be under his old familiar helmet. He advanced the throttle all the way and proceeded to climb again. It would be more economical on the gas if he could fly higher.

I'm going to enjoy this flight, he told himself, and see if I can get on top of the clouds.

Suddenly at 8,500 feet, he broke out of the clouds into the clear night. What a beautiful sight! There were stars all over the sky. A sliver of a moon was shining brightly off in the distance. Spontaneous praise burst from Paul's lips.

"Lord, how powerful you are!" he said, full of emotion. "How utterly powerful!"

Paul's mind went back by contrast to where he had just been captive. He thought of the darkness there — a darkness of soul far deeper than that of the night around him. He immediately felt sorry for those guerrillas, especially those who were "sucked into it" and indoctrinated against God. In a sense, they were the real captives. But they had chosen their way and the consequences which go with it.

More than ever, Paul was happy that he had chosen God's way and its accompanying blessings. He was even free physically now and up in the heavens praising God. Again he thanked Him for blinding the eyes of his guerrilla guards and deafening their ears. How utterly faithful He was!

There was time now to look back over the unbelievable and review it. His very nerve in trying to get out was not his normal human nature. He talked it over with his Creator who seemed so close up there under the stars.

"Thank You, Lord, for putting me in a circumstance where the only way out was to trust in You. Once again, You've shown me your power."

Paul's mind went back to I Peter 4:19 which had so inspired him two days earlier: *"...let them that suffer according to the will of God commit the keeping of their souls to him in well doing, as unto a faithful Creator."*

No earthly problem penetrated Paul's mind now — not even a worry about how to land in the dark. He felt so safe and secure up there in the hands of the "faithful Creator," in the expert care of the Creator of all those stars and the moon. His heart fairly blurted out utterances of praise, but words could not seem to express for him the wonderful presence of God he felt — so safe above that black jungle below him. He could only repeat, "Thank You, Lord!"

Paul was amazed anew at the confidence he had when he had stepped out of the mosquito net and had set out in the dark. He felt he had experienced "getting his feet wet" in a new way. But what was it that gave him that confidence he had not experienced before? Now he saw it all: It was when he caught a fresh picture of God from His Word — a reminder of who He was, is, and will continue to be.

"That's it!" he said out loud. "It was realizing that He never changes and that He lives in me! So why not trust Him and escape?"

Now he thanked God for each detail — even for not letting anybody snore, though that would have made it a bit easier. "It was so neat, Lord," he said, "for You to let me have the privilege of just walking by faith, trusting your Word, and 'getting my feet wet.' Thank you for bringing that to my mind, Lord, about the Israelites crossing the Jordan River and for encouraging me to get out from under the net and go. Otherwise I'd still be there!" The thought made him shudder.

No, it had not been a matter of "If it works out…fine; but if it doesn't…fine." Rather, it was as though he had a whole army (the guerrillas) coming after him, and he needed to get his feet wet, just like the Israelites with the Egyptian army coming behind them. No other way to go but forward!

Paul had further motivation, though, besides an army out to get him. He had information that he needed to get to the folks back at headquarters. He had been really burdened all this time for Tim and Bunny and Steve, wanting to believe that they were already free, yet afraid they were not. In that case, he sensed that what he knew about the guerrillas just might help in securing their release.

The steady drone of the engine gave him a grateful feeling. God had allowed him to get the plane out so that the missionary teams and Indians could have air service again. Paul felt he could now see God's overall reason for this. It was not just to save his own neck, but it was in God's plan and for His purpose that He had chosen to get Paul out *with the plane* — that He might be glorified.

Normally, in a situation like this, Paul knew he would have been nervous about the end of the flight; but he was surprised to find that he was enjoying it. A neat feeling, he thought, when the circumstances were contrary and impossible, to just *know* that God was going to work it out well.

By this time, he knew he must get down out of the clouds to get his bearings over a certain town. This would tell him if it was time to change headings. The town had an airstrip but was known as a hangout for guerrillas and cocaine-growers. He could not afford to land there! He had in mind two or three airstrips where he might land if he headed in the general direction of Lomalinda. He was grateful now for the extra gas he had taken on at *La Laguna* which had not been needed to make the air drop. God knew he would need it this morning.

Leaving the beautiful scenery above, he penetrated back down through the cloud layer into blackness again. Hopefully, there would be some lights visible in the town by which to identify it. His clock showed thirty minutes of flight behind him. Down he went, holding his heading closely, to an altitude of 4,500 feet. The town should be somewhere below him now unless wind had blown him off course.

Sure enough, there was a light far below in the darkness, and then another. Looking directly down through a hole in the clouds he could see the lights of the town and, at the same time, the telltale bend in the river that marked it for him.

"That's it!" he exclaimed; then, "Thank You, Lord, for opening up that hole!" Paul changed his heading and, from that point on, saw nothing but the pitch-black darkness. He could not afford the fuel to climb back up to the stars; he would run out within an hour.

By checking his navigation radios, he found the Villavicencio VOR to be working, so he set 185 degrees with the OBS. He would know when he was over Lomalinda when the needle centered on the VOR indicator while holding the 315-degree heading. From there, too, he should be able to see the lights of another town. He hoped to find a certain crop duster strip where it would be safe and flat all around.

The thought of a too-soon landing made him remove the tool box from under the seat. Anything can happen on a landing like this, he told himself, and I don't want that heavy thing smashing into my feet.

In time, the needle of the VOR indicator centered. But to his disappointment he could not see a thing but blackness. Sure enough, way on ahead he saw a glow from the lights of the other town, but the gas gauges told him he could never reach that far. Both were pegged on Empty. Not a light from Lomalinda could be seen nor any sign of the river which should have been off to the left.

"I have to get this thing down before it runs right out of gas," Paul talked to himself, knowing that, if the engine stopped, he would not have as much control or choice of a landing spot. He pushed the yoke forward and began a descent. Down at 2,500 feet, he turned on the taxi light. At 2,000 feet, he found himself enveloped in fog or cloud layer.

"Oops! I can't land in that stuff!" Quickly he pulled up on top of the cloud layer. He had to remember not to go down to zero, because he had set the altimeter arbitrarily at zero feet; but here the ground was higher.

Paul kept flying, with his taxi light shining on top of the cloud layer. Foolishly, he looked at the gas gauges again. Still empty!

"No sense in looking at those things!" he blurted out.

Soon, he noticed the cloud layer lowering. He continued to ride it down. The lights of a small village glowed up through the cloud layer off to the left. He turned toward it but could not spot an airstrip. The clouds were hanging low there, right over the houses and trees of the town.

No, I don't dare attempt a landing here, he reasoned, or I could hit a house and kill somebody.

He turned the plane away from the town, pulled back on the yoke, and climbed back up into the darkness on top of the cloud layer. He was back on his original course. Within moments, he saw that the cloud layer was breaking up and becoming lower and lower. Next, he could smell burnt *savana* or grasslands.

"Ha! Burnt *savana!*" He liked the familiar smell which indicated that ranchers were burning the old grass to provide new for the cattle. And for him, it spelled flat country close by.

Soon his taxi light spotted the ground and he could see brush, high clumps of termite nests and mounds of ant hills on the plains flashing past beneath him. It was anything but clear terrain. Some of the brush stood four to five feet tall. All around was pitch dark night except for what his taxi light showed up.

Suddenly some trees appeared. Instinctively, he pulled back sharply on the yoke. The plane responded beautifully, soaring up over the trees. Then easing down again, he lowered himself over the brush, searching for a landing spot.

Then more trees! Up and over again! The plane responded jubilantly now, as it was light — no cargo and no fuel!

For a flash, Paul wondered why he was not shaken. It would have been more like him to be perspiring, his throat all tightened with fear. Instead, he had a rare confidence that God was in control.

Unbelievable! he thought, the peace and calm God is giving me right now! He found he was actually enjoying it.

The little Cessna kept going on Empty over a stretch of *savana* that appeared to be long enough to land on, with no trees on it. Paul banked the plane around, wanting to make a 180-degree turn to set it down there. He was so low that he had to keep his eyes right out where his light was, and at the same time, on his instruments to keep from running into the ground. In the meantime, he lost the landing site! Quickly, he pulled up as more trees were coming at him.

Now he flew just above a fourth maze of tree tops, his taxi light assuring him of a safe distance, until he came to the edge of the trees. Simultaneously, the taxi light shone on a fence row.

"Aha! This should be pasture!" he concluded. "What better place for a landing!" Immediately, he chopped the throttle, pulled on full flaps, and eased down over the edge of those trees. Using the fence as a reference, he set the plane down on the ground in short order and applied the brakes as hard as he could. Quickly the plane came to a full stop and he turned off the motor.

"Thank You, Lord." Paul meant it deeply. He did not know where he was, but he was down on the ground safely — far removed from guerrilla territory.

9

Reunion

The little Cessna had landed in a field, fifty yards short of a swamp with palm trees. Once Paul turned off the taxi light and motor, all was pitch black. His immediate question was whether he had in any way damaged the plane on his approach between drifts of fog in the wee hours of the night. At least, he had heard no thump or bang. Cautiously, he opened the door and climbed out.

Feeling along the leading edges of the wing he checked all the way down around the tip. Then walking back, he felt the "tail feathers" and over to the other wing tip, down the leading edge, and back to the prop. He could not feel even one scratch! Again, he could only say, "Thank You, Lord."

Back he climbed into the cabin and checked the time on the instrument panel: 3:23 a.m. Time to rest a bit until dawn. He crawled over into the back seat and settled down.

Mosquitoes beat him to it, however, so he had to get unsettled and close the door and window. Try again!

Something else was keeping Paul from sleeping: wet, muddy pants, and mud both inside and outside his socks. He stirred again to take off his shoes and socks and try to scrape the mud out of them.

It felt so good to be sitting in that airplane waiting for dawn rather than on his four boards back in the guerrilla camp! His heart fairly burst with thanksgiving and praise to God as little by little the reality of his freedom got through to him. He was far too keyed up to sleep, so he decided to spend some time in prayer.

Steve, Tim, and Bunny were much on his mind. Were they free, too? And if so, Paul wondered who went in after them and brought them out. He wondered, too, about the Indians down there in Morichal. How were they faring now that the guerrillas had taken over the village? As Paul talked it over with God, he thanked Him especially for getting him out of the guerrilla camp without anyone being hurt or killed, so there would be no reprisals against the Mission. He knew the guerrillas might have it in for him for embarrassing them. "Lord," he prayed, "I'm confident You can continue to take care of me."

As soon as it was light, Paul climbed out of the plane to find out where he was, if possible. What he saw was a miracle in his landing. Just on the other side of the fence that he had used for a reference, there were about 250 head of cattle, all sleeping with the mist and fog coming in between them.

"Ooph!" he gasped. "Lord, You knew I couldn't have landed there!"

He walked around to the other side of the airplane and saw another fence that paralleled "his." On the other side of that fence was a stream, some trees, anthills, and erosion. He could not have landed there, either! Then he summed it up. God had put him down on a smooth pasture on the right side of each fence, hemmed in by trees at one end and a swamp with palm trees at the other. Half audibly, he put it into words, "That's precision! That's God!"

Shortly before radio time, Paul noticed a man on a horse riding in his direction. The closer he came, the slower he rode. No doubt he feared the plane was involved in drugs. Realizing his reluctance, Paul began to walk toward him and motioned for him to come, *"Por favor."*

When he arrived, Paul told him briefly that he had escaped from the guerrillas but had run out of gas. The man was very sympathetic, living himself under constant threat of guerrilla kidnappings for ransom.

Paul learned where he was in relation to the nearest town.

"Come with me to the ranch and have breakfast!" he invited.

Paul declined, as he was anxious to call on the radio.

"I understand," the man said. "I must go and get on with my chores. But I'll come back later to see if you're needing any help."

6:30 at last! The normal broadcast time for the Mission network. With much emotion, Paul got on the radio and tried to call Mary Cain. But the reception was poor, and there was a lot of static. Finally three or four radio stations which were monitoring the frequency joined in one by one to relay the message to Mary Cain and Macon Hare.

Only then Paul got it across that he had escaped, that he was out of gas, and that he did not know exactly where he was except for the name of the nearest town. Then he asked if they would request a favor of the folks from Lomalinda to bring him a few gallons of gas. Paul had dipped his tanks again with the dipstick just to double check, but both were dry.

As soon as communication was better, Paul asked Mary if she had heard anything from Steve, Tim, and Bunny.

"No, we haven't heard a thing since the day you left," she answered.

Paul's heart sank. He began again to worry, but God reminded him, Paul, didn't I get you out?

"Yes, Lord, You got me out. And I know You can get them out!" As he agreed with God, his heart was encouraged to trust Him for the release of the other three.

If Paul could only have seen what went on at the other end of his radio communication that morning! About twenty people were crowded into the senior Cains' house, listening closely for any word they might catch from Paul's actual voice. Someone had taken the word quickly to Pat, who ran out in her stocking feet.

She ran across the airstrip and the football field to get there, faster than she had run in years. "You could have outrun any of us!" said one young man when the communication was over.

Pat walked home with Grandma Poulsen. "Oh, Pat," the elder missionary said, "in the night, I was praying so much for Paul. God seemed to stop me praying for the *four* hostages for a while just to center my prayer on Paul. It was probably around midnight. I seemed to see him trying to escape, as though he were swimming."

"Oh, go on, Grandma," said Pat, "how could you see things like that in your prayer?"

"Pat dear, I was not dreaming. I was just sitting up on my bed praying, and God seemed to show me that Paul needed my help in prayer right then. So I prayed on until God gave me peace." It was too hard to explain how she had struggled in prayer for him, though God had assured her before that Paul would come back.

Both JAARS and TAC have emergency locator beacons and direction finders (DF) on their planes which would allow either to find the other within a certain range, if downed. So Paul turned on

"He could hardly see to land and park the plane."

the ELT transmitter and waited. It was not long before he heard the drone of an airplane and then of another.

Paul jumped out of the Cessna and was excited to recognize two JAARS helios headed his way. As soon as he was sure they had spotted him, he ran back, turned off the ELT and switched on his "com." radio, dialing in JAARS' frequency. He could hear Pilot Al Meehan saying he had him in sight. Then, "Is it safe to land down there?" Al asked.

"Yes, it's beautiful!" Paul responded. "Just a minute. I'll run out and step off an area for you and place a towel where you can touch down."

"Are you sure you'll be able to do that?"

"Why do you ask?" Paul wondered.

"Well, we've heard you have been shot."

"No, *negativo*. I have not been shot. I'm OK."

"Well, praise the Lord!" Al was satisfied.

Paul ran out toward the trees he had hopped over in the dark and checked the surface for anthills and holes within a distance he knew would be long enough for them to land in. He laid out his handy towel, then ran back toward the Cessna. Soon both planes were on the ground and parked alongside his. Al had brought the extra plane with a doctor and a stretcher plus a third pilot to fly the Cessna, thinking that Paul should be flown out on a stretcher.

Pat Dye and others greet Paul on his return to the finca

As all climbed out of their planes, they met each other halfway. These brothers in Christ wrapped their arms around Paul as though he had been their long-lost beloved brother. To Paul they represented *love* and *freedom*. Then they stood around while Al prayed, expressing their thanks to God for Paul's deliverance from the guerrillas.

Quickly they put fifteen gallons of gas into the wing tanks of the Cessna, and all took off for Lomalinda. The fog was already lifting, but the helios preferred to fly above it. Paul flew underneath, noting the terrain over which he had flown in the night while looking for a landing place. Most of it was too rough and difficult for an emergency landing in the dark. Once again, he was impressed with the greatness and power of God on his behalf.

At Lomalinda, Paul was met by a host of friends — brothers and sisters in Christ who had been praying, and now were so happy to witness the answer to their prayers. Many of them had awakened at midnight with a special burden to pray for Paul. No wonder they almost overwhelmed him with their welcome! He recounted his story for them, but very briefly, as he was anxious to get on home.

Before he left, however, the folks at Lomalinda treated him to a shower. Someone gave him a T-shirt, another a pair of socks, and so on. He left for the *finca* feeling much more presentable than when he had arrived.

Dear Uncle Paul Die,
I'm so glad that you came back
I missed you when gone.
I hope you have fun out
here now. I'm having fun in
school. How are you doind?
I'm doing fine. I am glad
that God can do a nother
mirical for my mom and Dad
and Uncle Steve aren't you?
verse I will say of the Lord ; He is my
refuge and my fortress: my God: in
Him will I trust. Psalm 91:1-2
Love
Cambie Cain

The folks at Mission headquarters, school children and all, were out waiting for Paul. The sight of them brought tears of joy to his eyes. He could hardly see to land and park the plane. Again, *love* and *freedom!* Someone called out to his wife, "You're first, Pat!" to which Pat responded, "No, we're all in this together!"

Paul headed straight for Pat and his son Luke, quickly including the rest. As he went the rounds of the embraces, he grabbed all four Estelles at once and urged them to keep believing God for the release of the other three. Similarly, with the two Cain girls. One of these, Cambie, the eight-year-old, wrote Paul a letter a few hours later, echoing what Paul had said to her, and confiding, "...I am glad that God can do 'a nother *mirical'* for Mom and Dad and Uncle Steve, aren't you?"

That afternoon, everyone met in the schoolhouse for two-and-one-half hours to hear Paul tell his story. Now and then, there were tears in his eyes, just as Grandma Poulsen had once anticipated. Then, he told graphically how he cleared off the wings of that plane — his eyes closed as though blind in the dark, his arms making the motions of a breast stroke to show how he cleared off the debris. Pat Dye recalled what Grandma Poulsen had seen in the wee hours of the night during intensive prayer. He was "escaping as though swimming." Pat got up from her seat and went back to where Grandma Poulsen was sitting.

"Oh, Grandma, please forgive me! I *do* believe God let you in on what was happening while you were praying!"

10

Peace in the Midst of Suspense

October 10 showed up on the calendar Bunny was keeping. That meant it was Kimberly Estelle's birthday. Steve thought of that dollhouse again. Why hadn't he worked on it earlier? There was nothing to do but pray that God would help Kimberly cope with the situation. Little did Steve guess how God would answer his prayer and send help in her time of need.

Many folks saw to it that Kimberly had a "happy birthday," complete with the dollhouse. But something had been missing. God had not yet answered prayer that her daddy would come back. She was very brave all day long, but at bedtime she started to cry. It was her eleven-year-old brother Jason who came forward to encourage her.

"Don't cry, Kimberly. We have to be strong. We have to realize that God lets things like this happen so that we'll pray more and read the Bible more and learn to trust Him!"

That morning in Morichal, Steve and the Cains had wondered what was going on among the guerrillas. Three new ones arrived by boat that day. One was the first woman guerrilla the missionaries had seen. It soon became clear she was the companion of one of the men. These talked with the others for some time, then entered the Cains' house.

"OK, pack a suitcase with a change of clothes, and get a hammock and a blanket," they ordered. "We're going downriver today."

By this time, the trio realized that as long as they were near the Puinaves they would be well treated. So leaving the village spelled only one thing to the American missionaries: They intend to kill us because they know we will not pay ransom! Perhaps they could put it off a while.

Steve spoke up. "Oh! But it's my daughter's birthday! I don't want her to hear that her dad was killed on her birthday!"

Bunny, much less fearful than at first, chimed in, "Yeah, if you take us out of here, you'll do anything because the Puinaves won't see you!"

The guerrilla leader became frustrated and went out to talk to the others. Immediately the trio in the house joined in prayer, "Lord, don't let it be today!" Steve did not try to tell God it was Kimberly's birthday, nor did Bunny or Tim argue before Him. It was just a "Please, Lord, don't let them take us today."

When the Puinaves became aware that these terrorists wanted to take the missionaries from the village, they became indignant and approached the guerrillas.

"We want you to leave those missionaries alone. Just leave them alone. These people have done nothing but good to us. They're the only ones that have!" Often they had told them this before, but Alberto tried again to intercede for them.

"I invited those folks here. They're my responsibility. If they're to leave, *I'm* the one that should send them out."

The guerrilla leader fought impatience and tried to calm him down, "No, don't worry, nothing is going to happen to them. They're under this investigation, and everything is going to be OK."

The love displayed by these quiet, reserved Indians was almost overwhelming for Tim and Bunny. Through the years, they had not always known what was going on in their minds. No doubt it was the exploitation at the hands of rubber workers and traders that had caused the Puinaves to keep their feelings suppressed.

In spiritual things, Tim had to work to draw them out in order to know how his teaching was coming across. More and more they began expressing themselves during or after the meetings. They showed amazement at God's power and His consistency in dealing with His people — His hatred for sin, but His love for man. They had known nothing before of the cunning of Satan in his desire to keep man from God. And they could hardly understand why God's people so often failed to respond to the One who made them and owned them. They now saw how distorted were their own ideas of God, to which they were in bondage.

Alberto had professed to be a Christian for twenty years and was a deacon in the church. He was the first in Morichal to understand why Christ had to die. He saw that his own Christianity was based on his good works. And soon there were others, like Chicho.

Downriver, where Tim met less often with three other groups, response came a little more slowly.

Once Tim had invited Larry Richardson, the linguist-translator, to join him in a two-week stint of Bible studies. At the end of one of Larry's messages, a very, very old man stood up.

> "I've got to say something! I understand! I've got to speak up!"
>
> Some "acting Christians" nearby drowned out his voice in the hub-bub that followed Larry's turn at teaching. "No, you don't understand! Sit down!"
>
> But the man was not to be turned away. He went on, and only Tim, seated behind him, caught his words, "I see it! I see it! When Jesus died on the cross, it was for *me!* He died for *my* sin!" Then he sat down.
>
> Tim leaned forward and talked with the man who glowed with an inner peace he had never shown before. Reassured, Tim could heartily say, "Then you are a child of God!"
>
> Then there was Carlos, who spoke up after Larry's lesson on Cain and Abel. Larry had explained how sin separates man from God and how man's condition is hopeless unless a substitute, acceptable to God, be sacrificed to bear the death penalty for him. Larry concluded by likening our hearts to the altars people used to build, explaining that today God sees upon our hearts whatever we offer to make us acceptable to Him. Abel had brought what God required for sin while Cain gave an offering of His own choosing.
>
> Suddenly Carlos stood up and said, "Now I understand." Then addressing his fellow Puinaves, he said, "You all know me and the good things I have done. I'm a deacon. I've opened the door for all the meetings. I've attended every morning prayer meeting. But I have just recognized that those are the things I have been thinking would make me acceptable to God. Yet in God's sight, those things are like Cain's offering. They're of my own choosing. Now I'm removing those things from my heart and replacing them with Jesus alone. He is the One who died to pay the death penalty for my sin. God is satisfied when He sees Him there just as He was with the lamb Abel sacrificed."

Both downriver and back in Morichal, Alberto's mother sometimes heard women testify of trusting Christ. So one night, in a meeting, she attempted to express herself.

"I know I'm a Christian because I go to all the meetings. I serve meals to the ones who come for conferences. And I...," she added a few more "works."

Alberto would not be fooled by that reasoning again. He interrupted.

"No, Mother, you don't understand yet. Just sit down, and we'll keep on teaching you what being a Christian is." And she soon saw he was right. She had yet to learn why Christ had to die, and why she needed a Saviour.

Alberto himself was very spontaneous with his gratefulness to God for saving him. "I was just *that* far from spending eternity in Hell!" he once said, as he held his thumb and forefinger apart to indicate the distance. Then one day, while Tim was helping him work on a new dugout, he stopped a minute in thought:

> "Timoteo," he said, "you or I could not just stand back and watch our son be killed like God did with Jesus. Yet *He* had the power to save Him! Do you know what that tells me? It tells me how *much* God loved me. And it tells me how terrible my sin is!"

Now Alberto was having a chance to express his love for God in the most practical way he knew — to "stick his neck out" on the Cains' behalf. Tim would not have to pray again, "Shake them up, Lord! Send something that would cause them to stand up for You."

The guerrilla leader returned to the house later on that morning. He had good news for the trio.

"OK, relax. We're not going to leave today."

The three missionaries thanked God for the "little miracle" He had so clearly worked for them. They were encouraged to believe God for more. That day they thoroughly enjoyed their Bible reading which taught them new things of God's power and of their own privileges in Him. They sang along with Tim's ukulele more joyfully than ever.

The next morning after breakfast, as they shared together new thoughts from their inmost souls, they were half expecting the leader to come in with an announcement again. And if so, it could mean the end. Tim began to see that they were not really prepared in heart for the worst to happen.

"Hey, do you know what I think our problem is? We're just not completely trusting the Lord for all this." Steve and Bunny agreed. Their attitude of the day before had been one of uneasiness which belied their deep-down trust in God.

"Lord, we've sinned," they confessed, "because *'whatsoever is not of faith is sin.'* We have not trusted you to do whatever you please with our lives."

Each one prayed. They deliberately surrendered themselves to God then and there for whatever might happen. After prayer, they felt assured that they had "come clean" with God and were resting in Him. Complete peace flooded each of their hearts. Even the commotion in Bunny's stomach subsided. At last, they felt they were ready for *anything*.

Immediately afterwards, the guerrilla leader came in.

"Get your stuff ready," he ordered. "We're going this time."

The news spread quickly among the villagers that the terrorists were taking Tim, Bunny, and Steve away from them. Perhaps they would never see them again. Men, women, and children — believers and unbelievers — gathered down at the riverbank to watch them load the dugouts. As they untied the boat from shore, it was too much for loyal hearts to contain. Puinaves, who rarely show emotion, cried unashamedly. Tim offered what little encouragement he could but was drowned out by the motors starting up. All the guerrilla leader could say was the refrain, "It'll be OK. It's only an investigation."

The little party of six guerrillas and three missionaries set out in a big dugout. They stopped for a couple of hours in the guerrilla camp nearby where most of them had been sleeping. Three more guards awaited them there. The guerrillas needed to collect their things, including a transmitter radio by which they had been keeping in touch with their superiors.

Meantime, two of the guards had gone on ahead to find a camp site a bit farther away from the village. When these returned, the whole group of twelve set out again in two boats. Little had been done to clear the site before all arrived, so both below and overhead, the jungle closed them in from the view of any who might pass by in plane or boat.

The guerrillas scouted out places for everyone. The kitchen and radio shelter were set up first, and sleeping places were marked off by a piece of black plastic strung over a rope. Two of the guards were assigned to set things up for the missionaries. They strung two hammocks for them between trees, but there was only one piece of black plastic left for a "roof" for the trio.

"Maybe you'd be better off with a bed," the guerrilla guards suggested.

So the two "scouts" went back to the village and brought the Van Allens' foam mattress and five by seven mosquito net with a "floor" in the bottom of it, which of itself made a little tent. Over this, they strung the plastic.

"It'll be all right if all three of you sleep in there, won't it?" they asked since by this time it was getting dark.

"Oh, sure!" they agreed, thanking God for each tiny bit of comfort.

"Tomorrow we'll fix up something else."

The mattress on the ground was only big enough for the Cains, so Steve had blankets folded up on the edge to function as a mattress.

Darkness fell all too soon. There was nothing to do but go to bed with the birds. One of the guards, however, had brought along some candles from the Cains' house. He set up a stick, like a lamp post, not far from the trio's mosquito net. By splitting the end of the stick, he was able to insert a candle and have a "street light" during the early part of the night. This, of course, did not give enough light for any reading, but it did help the guard on duty who had to be sure that the trio did not try to escape during that time. The flashlights shone in their eyes more frequently now in the jungle than back in the Cains' house.

The following morning, the abductors had nothing better to offer their captives in the way of sleeping quarters. So for lack of a piece of plastic, that "cocoon" became the home of the trio. Tim, who slept in the middle, had to keep his arms above his head to make enough room. Steve saw the humorous side of the whole situation.

"You know, my dad always taught me not to wear out my welcome," he said to Tim and Bunny, "so whenever you get tired of me, just let me know. I'll be glad to go home!"

During the daytime, the heat was stifling, so they sat outside on the ground or on any log they could find in spite of gnats and bugs. The guards had made a shelf of poles the night before to keep the Cains' suitcase off the ground. Now, at Tim's request, they also made a bench of poles for them to sit on.

When it rained, however, the mattress and bottom of the mosquito net became uncomfortably wet. The guerrillas fared likewise, having used palm leaves and brush for mattresses, though some had hammocks. They scouted around a bit and, two days later, cut out a higher spot farther back in the jungle, though adjoining the same site. Here the hostages were placed farthest away from the river in the camp set-up.

The daytime was spent much the same as in the village. The guerrillas were called at 4:30 for breakfast and then were off to their duties. The missionaries were served much later, then chose their own schedule. All three missed Tim's ukulele which had remained in the village. But they still sang, prayed, read the Bible, and talked, usually sharing what they were reading. At times, their hearts seemed to be literally overflowing with joy as Scriptures came alive in a new way. Their minds remained at rest in the midst of the suspense as to what would happen to them and when.

Bunny no longer had the distraction of fixing meals as she did back in the house, so the days seemed longer for her. The guerrilla cook did well with what he had — beans, rice, and often meat. The guards butchered a pig they had led or carried around for a couple of weeks; sometimes they had chicken, and a few times, fish. Tim was glad to go fishing one day with a couple of guerrillas who did not seem to have a knack for pulling them in.

Shortly after their isolation in the jungle, the leading guerrilla volunteered a bit of news.

"Capitán Pablo has escaped," he said, in a tone that was intended to impress his hearers.

"Is that right?" asked one of the missionaries.

"Yes, he escaped at night with only a little bit of gas in the plane. He probably crashed somewhere in the jungle. It's *impossible* for him to have landed anywhere safely in the dark."

To believe this or not was the question. There was no way for the three hostages to know more. Yet they continued to pray for Paul.

On October 15, the missionaries and guerrillas could hear a small plane land in Morichal. It took off again in record time. About forty-five minutes later, a boat pulled into the port of the jungle camp with two new guerrilla commanders, each in military uniform and each with a female companion. Their arms were more sophisticated than those of the guards.

One commander was to take over the guerrilla guards. There had been some bickering among the guards as to who was boss. ("You can't tell *me* what to do because you are of the same rank as I!") For identification purposes, Tim nicknamed this commander "Brass." He was of medium height, rather thin, and with tousled curly hair. His female companion took on the role of drill sergeant and proceeded to drill the guards, especially in the handling of guns.

The second commander, who had come on the boat, headed straight for the hostages. "I am here to take care of you and to see that you get back to your own people," he said. "I will turn you over to the Peace Commission when they arrive from Bogotá."

Steve, Tim, and Bunny looked at each other in unbelief. Yet they took on real hope with that announcement. Whatever the "Peace Commission" was, they had no idea, but it sounded good. Was it possible they would be freed without anyone paying ransom? They had prayed to this end. Now their thoughts ran wild. Things were really looking up.

At the same time, Brass asked the guards what they had confiscated of the Cains' things. They confessed to the obvious ones they were using and handed over things like tape recorders, Tim's radio, and most of the money that had been taken. Further, the commanders apologized for the way the three had been treated. No longer would they be accused falsely or told they were bad.

From this time on, the missionaries received special attention to the point of embarrassment. "Can we get you another pillow?" "Would you like some crackers?" (These, of course, would have been from the Cains' house.) Steve, Tim, and Bunny were not quite sure how to react to all this. They boldly asked two favors: First, could they have their food with less oil in the cooking? While the petition was well received, it seemed the cook still felt it tasted better greasy, so nothing more was said. They were grateful to be well fed. Secondly, could the guards try to avoid their eyes when shining their flashlights at night? The constant bright light right in their eyes had been quite disturbing. This request was happily granted although the frequency of the light flashes remained the same.

In an off moment at this time, Steve said something about his favorite food, pancakes. So the woman who did not seem to have an assignment invited Bunny to make some. After two pancake meals, she asked Bunny to teach her and was excited to have pancakes turn out well for her, also.

The three soon found that the commander in charge of them had another function. He lectured to them periodically with great gusto on the greatness of communism. These lectures earned him the title, "Professor." Intermingled with this brainwashing were pointers on the awfulness of capitalism. The soft-spoken manner in which he "taught" them was quite impersonal. The trio had no choice but to sit and dutifully listen.

Soon after his arrival, Brass told the missionaries, "Capitán Pablo has arrived safely back in Villavicencio."

Brass paused. Did his listeners really grasp the trauma of this fact for the guerrillas? Why else were they softening in attitude towards the trio? And why else was his partner-in-command preparing them for possible exit to the outside world? Then he addressed Steve.

"You tell your friend Pablo that he lied to me! He said he had only a little bit of gas in his tank!" Brass, like the rest of the guerrillas, saw no other way for Paul to have done the impossible. The three hostages, of course, had no way of knowing how and where this man had talked with Paul. Steve knew he was not one of the two who flew away with Paul from the Morichal airstrip. But he had not seen the commander Paul picked up on the way to his "prison camp." What Steve caught, though, was the intimation from Brass's remark that Steve was to be talking with Paul again!

Shortly after the arrival of Professor and his friends, a big plane flew overhead and sounded as though it landed in Morichal. Then the telltale clatter of helicopters came from the Morichal direction also. The guerrillas became excited. They seemed to think the army had arrived. The commanders put on a special guard to stand watch over the missionary hostages. Until now, they had not put a guard between them and the jungle, thinking that on first arrival they had scared these foreigners away from the jungle as a way of escape. ("The jungle is dangerous. The only way out of here is by river.")

The special guard stationed himself in the jungle behind the missionaries. There he stayed all day watching, with his gun ready to defend the hostages from any intruders. Two others took their places deeper into the jungle, still behind the captives. They only came out to eat, returning quickly the same way, instead of staying around the camp. The rest of that day and night they maintained their special alert. It seemed that they expected soldiers to be hiding in the jungle. After a few hours they heard the helicopters take off. But clearly, the big plane was staying overnight.

Early the next morning, October 16, Professor told the missionaries to pack up.

"We're going to leave for a new camp site farther away," he told them. "We want to protect you from the military! But we won't leave until the army does."

Steve volunteered a bright idea. "If we are really to be taken out, why don't you take us back to Morichal and let us fly out with the army plane?"

"No way! They'd kill you and then say that *we* did it!" This was his way of reminding Steve that guerrillas were mortal enemies of the army and the government.

No one left camp that morning until they heard the army plane leave Morichal at about 6:30. Then captors and captives set out for the new site, fifteen minutes away and up a little creek. They carefully placed a guard at the mouth of the creek and another back in the jungle area behind the camp.

This time, the guerrillas fixed the "cocoon" up off the ground on poles as they did to their own beds. Now when it rained, no one got as wet as they had previously. The only problem Tim found was where to settle so that a pole could fit in comfortably with the bones of his back!

It rained that very day. When the rain stopped, there were too many gnats, so the trio sat inside the cocoon, in spite of the heat. They heard some guerrillas take off in a boat to points unknown.

"You know," Bunny said to the other two, "wouldn't it be nice to have a soda pop? ...an ice-cold soda pop? But where in the world would anybody get ice around here?" She would be satisfied with just the soda pop!

When the boat returned, the guerrillas marched up to their captives and presented them with three grape soda pops from Venezuela!

"Wow! Thank you!" the trio called out in one voice. Bunny was overwhelmed. "I hadn't really asked the Lord for it!" she told Tim and Steve. "God just knew we needed that." Tiny as it might have seemed in others' eyes, it was a real encouragement to the three — even without ice. They thanked God for it together.

"You should have asked for the ice, too!" quipped Steve.

Bunny was encouraged later to ask God for another miracle. She had been reading alone inside the cocoon, going through the Psalms and, in fact, on her way to reading through the whole Bible. But the cocoon was so hot and muggy, and she couldn't face the gnats outside.

"God," she prayed, "I know I'm not worthy. It's not because of how good I am or anything like that. But God, Your Word says You're rich in mercy, and it's *so* hot. Lord, would you just show me your mercy now and send a breeze?"

God did. Right away a cool breeze came along that encouraged Bunny's heart. She told the men, "Do you know why we got this breeze? 'Cause I asked Him and He did it!" Bunny was thrilled with the "little miracles."

On a Saturday night, after nine days in the jungle, Tim found himself losing his usual optimism. But he knew where to turn.

"God," he prayed silently, "I'm a father of two girls. And I know there are times when my girls need to be held, need special attention, need to touch me, and need me to touch them. Well, that's the way I feel myself right now, Lord. I need You to touch me. I need You to do something special for me because I just feel insecure."

About this time Steve spoke up, "Tim, what are you thinking?" And Tim freely confided what his prayer had been.

Nothing special happened that night.

The next morning the camp was up before dawn, followed later by the birds, but not the usual two or three birds here and there. Steve was the first to see what was happening.

"Tim, here's your answer! Look at the choir of birds that has come to join us for a Sunday morning service!"

A choir it was! Big birds and little birds were sitting on the branches of trees all around them. Just as if led by a heavenly choirmaster, the birds sang and chirped all around the three hostages, looking right at them, almost nodding as they sang or even croaked. The missionaries first counted about twelve classes of small birds, besides parrots, toucans, and even a big black and white turkey buzzard. Next the count rose to twenty-six classes of birds.

This was enough for Tim. God *had* heard him and had certainly done something special. The birds hardly moved for several hours, except to hop occasionally from branch to branch. As they sang, they sounded like a well-organized recording of a singing birds' menagerie. The trio "joined them" in a worship service, singing their songs in Spanish, English, and Puinave.

At 12 o'clock the birds all left. No special gathering of birds appeared the next day, and none the next.

"Look at that choir of birds...for a Sunday morning service!"

The missionaries wondered if they would come around for a "Wednesday night prayer service," but there was no sign of them.

The following Sunday, there was the bird choir again! This time it was more numerous than before — all singing, chirping, croaking. And again, they stayed around until noon. The guerrillas "couldn't care less," when the missionaries drew their attention to the birds. But Tim was thrilled, as were Bunny and Steve. These "little miracles" spoke more than words could say of a Father who wanted to reach out and touch them, and who was touched by them.

11

"Footwork" and a Secret Mission

Paul kept somewhat incognito back in Villavicencio. He had taken pains immediately upon landing at the *finca* to conceal the Cessna as much as possible and had cautioned all Mission members not to tell of his escape. He was concerned that this news be kept away from the media while they sought ways and means of persuading the guerrillas to release his three missionary companions peacefully. Certain parties who had let the news leak to the media back in the United States were requested to cap it in every way possible, to let the guerrillas function on their own.

Macon Hare, Jr., had done a great deal of groundwork before Paul escaped. From Civil Aeronautics, word had gone out to other pilots to be on the lookout for the Cessna. When it was deduced that it was in the hands of terrorists, word passed on quickly but quietly to other authorities.

Macon's duties were multiplied — seeing authorities for advice, answering questions from the area and farther away. Ken Newton, one of the teachers at Fusa, left his work in capable hands and responded to the emergency, also. Lindy Drake, who had had to abandon his own work in a tribe because of guerrillas, pitched in to help. He took up his post in Villavicencio where the Mission phone was "ringing off the hook" and took over many of Macon's normal duties. This kept Macon free to tend to the emergency.

One furloughing missionary made it a point to call any others on furlough from Colombia. This paid off in more prayer and in offers to help. Two men returned, leaving their families still on furlough at home and quickly found the niches they could fill to relieve the situation. One of these, Dan Germann, with a gift for public relations, accompanied Macon in Villavicencio and Bogotá.

Together, these men ferreted out information on where they should go for advice and what steps they should take to try to secure the release of Steve and the Cains. Sometimes things looked hopeful. Then again, their task looked impossible. But hourly, more folks back home were being added to the list of intercessors.

With Paul's escape, the whole picture took on some tangible proportions. Paul had with him the evidence needed to show that the very group that had ambushed him was one of a few guerrilla groups which had a Peace Treaty with the government. This breach of treaty, of course, would give the army freedom to go in and deal with the guerrillas. But the Mission did not want the army to enter. They prayed daily now that the guerrillas themselves would release their three fellow workers.

Macon and Paul went to Bogotá to report and to get advice from the American Embassy. The Embassy promised to cooperate in every way possible and made suggestions as to whom they should see for help. But there was actually very little the Embassy could do without interfering in the internal affairs of the country.

While in Bogotá, Paul told his story to an American friend who seemed rather unbelieving about God's role in the whole matter. He was telling the part about his failure to get out a night earlier. Al Meehan, the JAARS pilot, happened to be in the same place in Bogotá at the time. He spoke up and corroborated Paul's account as being the hand of God. He turned to Paul.

"Paul, you know what? I thought of this the other day after you first talked to me about what happened: It was just of the Lord that you didn't get out that first time, because all around Lomalinda and the whole area where you landed, we had nothing but storm — lightning, thunder, and rain. There was no way you could have landed out there that night! God just didn't want you out that night."

Another "Thank You" went up to God from Paul's heart.

Then Al continued, including the American friend as he addressed Paul. "I woke up that Wednesday morning at about 4:30 and just felt that something good was going to happen that day. I began reading in Psalm 91."

At this point, Al began quoting verbatim the last three verses of the Psalm:

> *"Because he hath set his love upon me, therefore will I deliver him: I will set him on high, because he hath known my name.*

"He shall call upon me, and I will answer him: I will be with him in trouble; I will deliver him, and honor him.

"With long life will I satisfy him, and shew him my salvation."

Al clarified for the American friend what he saw in the passage. "God delivered Paul because Paul set his love upon God; because Paul knows the Lord." The friend did not know what to say in the face of a story so unbelievable. But as Al was leaving, he reassured Paul, "That's why you got out — because you love the Lord and you hold Him high in your life. He set *you* on high."

Early in the morning of October 13, nine days after the capture of the Cains, Macon found a note that had been shoved under the door of the Villavicencio Mission home during the night. The "note" turned out to be quite a document. It was the long-expected ransom note. But it did not claim to be from the F.A.R.C. The whole document claimed to be written from Morichal by a smaller Marxist group led by "Ricardo Franco," and was dated October 9.

The document began, "We have in our custody four foreign missionaries of American nationality: Mr. and Mrs. Tim Cain, Captain Paul, and Mr. Steian Estil [*sic*]." Clearly the news of Paul's escape on the morning of the 9th of October had not caught up with the "powers that be" among the guerrillas. Then followed some absurd and gross accusations as to what the missionaries had done to exploit the Indians, implying that they, the guerrillas, must punish such crimes.

The ransom requested was equal to about $131,000, just for the release of "Mrs. Cain who was in delicate health." It indicated that they would consider negotiating for the plane and the other three missionaries after the first ransom was taken care of.

The note gave instructions as to how to announce in code by radio that the Mission agreed to pay it, insisting that they keep quiet about the matter to the authorities. (Silence before the authorities had been the keynote to the success of many ransom transactions. Business companies and people anxious for their loved ones would pay quietly, promising secrecy even on release. Thus, kidnapping was very much on the increase.)

Paul could understand why Felipe had tried to tell him that they were not of the F.A.R.C. but of the E.L.P. Felipe had seen immediately that they would get in trouble with the Peace Commission for the kidnapping if the truth were known. But now they were supposed to believe it was a different group yet — the Ricardo Franco!

According to Mission policy, as soon as any ransom note was received, the families of the kidnapped had to leave the country. This was to avoid possible harassment to them. The American Embassy cooperated beautifully with passport matters to help Betsy take her three children and Mary Cain take Tim and Bunny's two girls home. Any authorities they needed to see were most helpful.

That the guerrillas had done the capturing for ransom purposes was what had been feared right along. Now the Mission knew it for sure. But who would have thought they would drag it out to demand ransom for only one at a time? This all called for serious thinking on the part of the Mission leaders. So Macon called Sanford, Florida, and requested that a member of the Executive Committee come down and confirm some decisions that seemed inevitable.

Mel Wyma and Duane Stous, both of missionary experience, responded to the call. They flew down to Bogotá the next day. Their own hearts were in turmoil over the whole matter. What could they do? But God encouraged them to hope and trust in Him. Psalm 64 seemed to point straight to the terrorists; then, reading on through to Psalm 65:5, they found inspiration — words of confidence in God to do the impossible.

> *They encourage themselves in an evil matter: they commune of laying snares privily; they say, Who shall see them?*
>
> *"They search out iniquities; they accomplish a diligent search: both the inward thought of every one of them, and the heart, is deep.*
>
> *"But God shall shoot at them with an arrow; suddenly shall they be wounded.*
>
> *"So they shall make their own tongue to fall upon themselves…*
>
> *"And all men shall fear, and shall declare the work of God…*
>
> *"The righteous shall be glad in the LORD, and shall trust in him; and all the upright in heart shall glory."*
>
> *"By terrible things in righteousness wilt thou answer us, O God of our salvation…"* (Psalms 64:5-10, 65:5).

Macon, Paul, and Ken met the two at the airport and were encouraged with their arrival. The first evening of their visit was spent in prayer together, as was a part of the next morning. Still it was not clear what they should do. Then they saw they must just go forward a step at a time. They would go along believing

La Laguna, *the lagoon where the missionaries had built houses on stilts to be less vulnerable to the wild Macú Indians*

that God would bring to their minds in different ways what lead to follow next.

After reporting in at the American Embassy and following a few possible leads as to what influential person they could visit, they went on down to Villavicencio to join Lindy who was getting bad news. There was turmoil in the country, rebels versus army, which did not make the Mission's situation any easier.

Then followed committee meetings, when some major decisions were made. For one, they must pull the missionaries out of three different tribes which were within easy access of the guerrillas. The most heartrending of these was the Macú tribe. It had taken so many years, with constant danger and at so much risk, to secure the friendship and trust of the Macú. Then, being a completely monolingual tribe, it had taken much time to reduce their language to writing. And now, just when the missionaries were getting along beautifully with them — *pull out?*

Rich Hess was flown out from La Laguna during this time to have his visa renewed. He brought news which put the seal on that decision. It had happened during his time in the jungle with Larry Dye:

Paul Dye with three of the Macú Indians

A motorboat of young men and one woman had made its way up the "Macú Creek" into La Laguna. Mike Gleaves and his family could hear the motor for almost two hours as it wound its way in from the big river. Mike became suspicious that it was guerrillas since anyone coming in to see *them* could only come by plane. Often, the missionaries heard motorboats and cocaine barges go up and down the river itself at some distance; still, no one had reason to come up the creek into their little lagoon where they lived in a house on stilts above the water.

Mike sent his wife and two girls in the boat to an agreed-upon hiding place in the jungle while he alone met the boat.

"We came to visit Dan Germann and Paul Dye," the visitors said.

Years had passed since Dan had left the Macú work, being transferred to the Fusa training center. And Paul had only been in and out as pilot. So it was clear to Mike that these folks were just grasping at names as an excuse to find out what went on there. Mike did not invite them into the house. He let them know that the men they asked for were not there and that the Macú were easily frightened by strangers. They had had tragic run-ins with intruders in the past.

"Very well," was the response. And the boat left

Paul became disheartened over this news. He felt sure that Mike's visitors were guerrillas. So the Macú also were to be deprived of their

Larry Dye, Andrés Jimenez, Lisa Dye,
a friend, and Luke Dye visit the Macú.

chance to hear the Gospel? He had agreed with the committee that the missionaries must pull out temporarily but did not realize the danger was that close. And when the missionaries abandoned La Laguna, the cocaine-growers would take over the airstrip since they had long ago asked to use it. This would give freedom to the guerrillas.

Rich, on hearing that he must pull out of the Macú work, was shaken. He had been so left out of the news while with the Macú that he and Larry did not even know of Paul's capture till Paul had already escaped. Then the radio had gone silent. Rich had only come in for his visa now because a plane was taking Mike's family out.

So Rich must leave, just when he had been thanking God for the increasing trust relationship between the Macús and the missionaries! He suggested to the committee that perhaps he could live alone with them inland, cut off from supplies. But Rich was gently reminded that usually, after two weeks away with the Macú, he would come out sick. This he could not deny. Finally he came to see that God could open up some other place to reach the Macú. Now, how could he get back to tell *them?*

The other main decision which had to be made that day was not too hard to make but harder to carry out. On advice of one of the authorities with whom they had talked, they decided to write a letter to the F.A.R.C. rather than answer their ransom note by radio. They would let them know that the Mission would never pay ransom and would try to get them to release the captives.

It had been suggested that once the letter was composed, Paul could fly over Morichal and drop copies there and at the other airstrip where the hijackers had taken him. All were a bit nervous about having Paul do this, even Paul himself. So the manner of delivery was left undecided.

Meanwhile, they set to work to write the letter. Six of the men were involved. Six different ideas came to the fore. There was confusion as to what should be said. They were conscious of the fact that what they put in that letter could mean either the death or the release of the prisoners. But after an entire afternoon, they came up with it, trusting that God had led them.

Now, how should copies of the letter be delivered? They knew there were guerrillas in Villavicencio since the ransom note had been slipped under the door. But they had no idea who the guerrillas were. Then, too, some friends of the Mission had teenage relatives who had joined the guerrillas. But one could never reach them. And if they could, how long would it take them to go by river to Morichal? So for certain it seemed the solution would be for Paul to fly a secret mission to those places.

Duane Stous took Paul aside. "Paul, how do you *really* feel about taking these letters?"

"Look," Paul said, "I feel a whole lot more concerned about that Macú situation than I do about flying those letters over Morichal!" Whereupon, Duane saw that Paul had a heart to do whatever had to be done, and all became satisfied with the arrangement.

Rich was greatly concerned to get back to La Laguna, but the Cessna had not budged since Paul's escape, and JAARS was not flying anyone into that area. Rich wanted to get back once more and try to find the Macú to let them know what was happening. He did not want them to run into danger when they would come out at La Laguna to see the missionaries, nor did he want them to feel the missionaries had abandoned them of their own accord.

It was arranged, then, for Rich to fly with Paul on his secret mission, help with the letters, and be dropped off at La Laguna where Larry and Mike were waiting. Rich would be able to hunt

Men of F.A.R.C.

As directors of New Tribes Mission, we believe that it is very important that you understand that we are missionaries and we never involve ourselves in political activities. Our concern is always for the good of the community, and we never enter tribal areas without an invitation from the Indians. Our main priority is the teaching of truths from the Holy Scriptures. The Indian chooses voluntarily, of his own will, if he desires to follow the spiritual teaching we show him from the Word of God, the Bible. Any one of the communities in which we work will verify that the goal of the Mission is to seek for the good of all. Also, they can verify the fact that we do not profess any political philosophy. Therefore, the accusations you have made about bombing and attacks on the Indians lack any credibility. We have no ties with the narcotic police, nor the military organizations, nor politicians of Colombia. Please believe us.

We direct this letter to F.A.R.C. and not to Ricardo Franco. On the basis of the reliable information that we have received from our co-worker, Paul Dye, the pilot of the plane you hijacked and who escaped from your watch, we know that some guerrillas, co-workers of yours, told him that they were with F.A.R.C., and for this reason we believe that our missionaries are in your keeping. We understand that you tried to correct this mistake by saying that you are from Ricardo Franco, because if the Colombian people found out that you are responsible for the kidnapping, it would endanger their confidence in your sincerity and good intentions. It would equally endanger the process of truce that is very advantageous for you.

Every member of the New Tribes Mission is dedicated to the work of the Lord. Several years ago Tim and Bunny Cain and Steve Estelle, along with the rest of our missionaries came to an agreement that we would never pay ransom. Bunny, Tim and Steve surrendered themselves into the Hands of God long before any guerrillas appeared in that region. We want you to know that you are responsible before the Living God, the God of the Holy Bible, for having taken His servants as prisoners. They do not represent any political philosophy, only that of the King of Kings and Lord of Lords, the Lord Jesus Christ.

We see in your communication prejudice against the missionaries based on their nationality. If all Colombians who live out of the country were to be judged by the illegal activities of some, then it is the same injustice to suppose that all North Americans that work in Colombia are bad. The truth is that the missionaries of the New Tribes Mission are citizens of many countries, and they work here in Colombia as residents of this country. The New Tribes Mission International membership consists of Colombians, Brazilians, Canadians, Filipinos, Australians, Dutch, English, North Americans and others.

Tim has involved himself with the socio-economics of the Puinave Indian community. At his own expense he helps them medically, even to the point of asking for emergency flights for the sick. He has never been indifferent to the needs of those people, nor has he ever exploited them in any way. To the contrary, he has shown a spirit of love and sacrifice. This can be verified by talking with the Puinave people.

Taking the lives of these three missionaries would be counterproductive for you. Public opinion would be in favor of the victims. We are doing everything possible to avoid publicity of this situation with the purpose of giving you the opportunity to set them free. We are convinced that the difficult circumstances in this lovely country of Colombia should have a solution, but not with the shedding of innocent blood.

Attentively,
NEW TRIBES MISSION

up the Macú, give his painful message, and then help Mike pack up for the evacuation.

Gasoline would be a problem. Since the trip was to be completely secretive, they would have to get a couple of barrels of gas without taking the plane to the airport. This was no easy task. Because of the cocaine industry, anyone buying gas had to register the amount, for whom, and, if for a plane, the destination of the flight.

Just when that situation looked impossible, God opened up an avenue they had never before used, and they received permission to get gas quite legally without disclosing Paul's mission.

Paul, then, without announcing his departure to anyone, set out with Rich on the morning of October 20. They had prepared eight letters for Morichal and eight for the landing strip where Paul had first taken the guerrillas. (It would be too far to go to the place where Paul had been kept captive.) Each letter was in a plastic bag weighted down by a potato. Eight letters were to be dropped from an open bag all at once over each target destination.

Not a soul was present in Morichal, not even a dog. But the letters hit dead center in the Indian village. In the other place, half an hour away, where Paul had been given the lemonade, there were people present. Here the airdrop hit the middle of the runway, and they saw someone run for one of the letters. They could only ask God to cause the letter to help so that their three co-workers would be released.

Back they headed, over Macú territory, to La Laguna. Paul left Rich there, chatted a bit with Mike Gleaves, then picked up his son Larry and headed back to the *finca*. Larry was sick with malaria and glad to be taken home. Paul, too, went to bed for some days with malaria, just as he had predicted his first night in the guerrilla camp.

Rich and Mike then made plans for final evacuation. Two JAARS planes were due to come in three days. Mike would pack all the valuables, especially the language and culture equipment and as much of everyone's household goods as possible. This would include what belonged to the Conduff family, then on furlough, and to Andres Jimenez, Rich's Colombian partner, who was out on sick leave. The choosing would be neither an easy nor a happy job for Mike.

Rich set out for the Macús over a familiar trail, then had to branch off on a different trail he had only covered once when the

Macús guided him. Now, without a guide, and with his mind on the future of the Macús, he came to some clearings he had never seen before. He soon realized he was lost. In trying to correct himself, he became even "more lost." This was almost as scary for Rich as the guerrillas were for Steve and Paul on the Morichal airstrip. Twice he stood and prayed, and waited and listened. There were always the hostile Macús to be on the lookout for, those who had not yet come out with the friendly group. Then, too, the jungle held many other dangers.

Finally after a private time with God, Rich chose a trail here and a fork there, even against his better judgment at times, until finally he came to a big tree he recognized; then he knew where he was. But when he arrived at the old camp site, no one was home. Six hours had passed, but he traveled still farther. Suddenly he heard a noise beyond the sound of monkeys nearby.

There ahead, sticking up from behind a bush was a painted, red face and a blow gun. Rich froze.

"Who are you?" he said in the Macú language, adding, "I am Monicaro (their version of Ricardo)."

No answer.

"Are you Wayneda'?" Rich looked straight at him.

That brought an answer quickly.

"No!" And one of Rich's good Macú friends stepped out from behind the bush, all curious. "What are you doing here? Were you alone on the trail? How did you get here?"

As best he could, Rich told him he had been lost, but that his Father (pointing upward) had directed him out of it and had put him back on the trail. Then Rich followed his friend to "the gang" who were then living well off the trail where Rich never would have found them. Before sleeping that night, Rich explained his mission. He told them what had been happening — quite understandable to the Macús, who had lost relatives to unfriendly "people with clothes" through the years. Further, the Macús had been perplexed when "Paul's plane" had not passed overhead on the return from Morichal on October 5 after their air drop. They had watched it, along with Larry and Rich in the clearing, where they cleaned a wild pig for dinner; and they were as excited as Larry and Rich over what the air drop package contained — mail from home and food treats.

The next morning, twelve of the group accompanied Rich back to La Laguna to pick up things that Mike and Rich wanted to share.

There would be food and other things that the missionaries could not take along as they were evacuated.

The Macús did not want to see the missionaries go, though they themselves knew it was dangerous around La Laguna. Cocaine-growers had given them enough scares already. Now they kept saying to Rich and Mike, "I'll miss you." "I'll miss you." They had become like family to the missionaries. How it hurt Rich and Mike not to be able to fully express the message they had really come to give them!

When the planes came to evacuate the missionaries, Rich flew out with the first load. Mike and the pilot were halfway loaded for the last trip when they heard a motorboat once again coming up their creek towards La Laguna. They looked at each other. It was enough to make both of them thank God they were on their way out. It could hardly be anyone but guerrillas! Fortunately it would take more than an hour for the boat to reach them.

When the half-loaded plane tried to pull out, they found it stuck in the mud. Mike and the pilot tried one way and another, pushing, pulling, and finally shoveling around the ailing wheel for almost half an hour. Every moment was punctuated with sounds of the intruding motor, the volume increasing and decreasing through the jungle as the boat wound its way around bends in the creek.

Finally the plane took off with part of the load left behind. The last Mike saw of his home was a few once-cherished possessions blown into the bushes by the force of the propeller. Material things had suddenly become quite dispensable. The plane motor silenced the awful, menacing drone of the motorboat which certainly spelled no good for any missionary inhabitants at La Laguna.

12

Hope Against Hope

On the first Sunday of the bird choir, October 20, another sound attracted the attention of the trio. They heard an airplane overhead that sounded different from the other planes they had heard. Steve, with his keen ear for motors, felt that it sounded unmistakably like the Mission's Cessna.

What could be going on? If indeed it was Paul up there, he would certainly not land. The drone of the plane soon died away, and they were left with their questions.

The following day, Professor returned from a trip to Morichal and began some interrogating.

"When you folks were first detained, what did they tell you?"

"Well," Tim replied, rather bored with the question, "they told us they were from the F.A.R.C."

"They did? They didn't tell you they were from the Ricardo Franco group?"

"No," Steve put in, "they never mentioned the Ricardo Franco group. They said right away, 'You are being detained by the F.A.R.C.'"

"How does your Mission use the plane to help the Indians?"

Steve tried to answer this one with specifics from what he had seen on his trips with Paul during the previous three months. There had been clear cases of using the plane to help Indians. These he recounted to Professor.

"What do you really teach the Indians?"

Tim had no problem with this one. He had freely given himself to the teaching of truths in the Holy Scriptures. But why should Professor be asking all this "old stuff" again?

Soon the commander seemed satisfied — as though the three had passed some test. He reached in his pocket and pulled out an envelope which he allowed them to look at.

"This letter," he said slowly, "is addressed to the F.A.R.C. from your Mission Headquarters. Notice on the top of the letter that it says 'URGENT URGENT URGENT' three times, no doubt because there are three of you." He paused, as though to let it sink in. This fact, for some reason, had impressed Professor greatly. Then he handed it to Tim.

"Read it out loud!" he ordered.

Tim did so, with Bunny and Steve all ears. They found in it some of the very answers they had just given Professor during his interrogating. Yes, the plane was used often to help the Indians. No, they had never been told that the guerrillas were of the Ricardo Franco group. Always it had been the F.A.R.C.

The whole letter — the tone of it, the truth of it — was a great lift to the three captives. It was something tangible, at last, that they could believe after being so long with folks whose word they had to question. Between the lines, they sensed love and concern, and they knew that prayer was going up to God on their behalf.

"Oh, God," they said in prayer that night, "Thank You for *Your* love. Thank You for the prayers of our loved ones. We pray that You'll help each of them to cope with the situation and be closer to You because of it. Work out Your will for us just so You get the glory!"

The following day, Brass and his female companion went over to where Bunny was sitting. They had a plan in mind for her.

"Vamos, señora," they said, "you're going with us."

Immediately, Bunny became nervous, wondering what was up. Then they added, "Want to go and see your family?" They had been referring to the Puinaves as the Cains' "family" for some time now. No doubt it sounded good also on the radio where almost everything was given in code.

Bunny felt they were sincere and had no hesitation. "Surely!" she responded. Tim and Steve were only sorry they were not invited.

"Well, we're going to take you up there. They think you're dead, but we're going to show them you're not, so let's go."

When the boat arrived in Morichal, Bunny and the guerrillas were disappointed to find only two families and part of another. The rest had gone and were not planning to return.

Bunny moved only at the command of the guerrillas at first. Then the woman guerrilla said, "Go greet your people."

But the guerrillas accompanied her. Bunny was not allowed to visit with them alone. Everything that she spoke in Puinave had to be interpreted for the guerrillas. They themselves spoke in Spanish to the Indians and found they were not being understood. So they had Bunny get across in Puinave some things they wanted to say.

"Tell these people the reason you're still in the jungle is that the Peace Commission hasn't arrived yet, and we cannot turn you over to your people until they come. Tell them you're OK." Bunny as yet had no idea what the Peace Commission was, and certainly, the Puinaves did not know. But she did her best to interpret into her not-quite-fluent Puinave.

Then, addressing one of the men, the guerrillas ordered, "Go downriver and get the other villagers. Tell your people that if they'll come back, we'll bring the other two foreigners. Tell your captain to come up because they're alive! We haven't killed them. We haven't done anything to them. They're just living in the jungle, and they're OK."

On their part, the Puinaves explained why most of the group had left. "We couldn't stand it around here without you," they said. "Most of our people went downriver to have 'the Lord's Supper' with the believers down there."

Bunny went back to the guerrilla camp that night thrilled with her visit. She greatly encouraged Tim and Steve with the bits of news she took back. Her commanders had allowed her also to pick up certain articles that would be useful in camp, including Tim's little ukulele. These homey things meant a lot to the prisoners after they were used to doing without.

Tim was listening to a Spanish broadcast that night. Suddenly, his eyes opened wide as he heard his own name. The broadcaster went on to say that guerrillas were holding three missionaries and asking 20 million pesos (roughly $130,000) for Bunny. He could not believe it.

"Hey!" he called out to Professor, "What's this?" He passed on what he had just heard. "You said you were not holding us for ransom."

"Oh, really? Is that what they said? Don't worry, it's probably some other group trying to take advantage of the situation you're in. Don't forget you have *not been kidnapped* by the F.A.R.C. You have been *detained* by us for your own protective custody."

Tim and the other two were left with their thoughts for a while but decided to take Professor's word for it. The evidence was in the decided change in the way they were being treated since the news of Paul's arrival back at the *finca.* So they dismissed the thought of ransom.

On October 25, it seemed that the guerrillas were letting up on the heavy guarding. Eight of them packed up their things and left for some other assignment. About the same time, the only four who remained took the trio back to Morichal for a visit.

Since Bunny's visit there, several chiefs had come back. These had demanded to see all three of the missionaries. Alberto and Chicho were there. There were two chiefs from another village, and yet another from a different place — all lives that had been touched by Tim's ministry.

Alberto immediately explained to Tim why he had left the village.

"Up here, I couldn't eat any more, thinking of you out there with those people," he said.

News passed back and forth between them until they were caught up with each other and their immediate interests. Tim was very encouraged by their attitudes. They were meeting together regularly. They were teaching others. Always, they were calling on God to release the prisoners.

"Oh, you will be set free," Alberto said, "because we have prayed!"

Alberto told the trio what had happened the day the army landed in Morichal, just a few days after the guerrillas had cleared out of the village with the missionaries.

"There were lots of soldiers!" he said. "They asked if we knew you, and we told them we sure did! They wanted to know where you were. We had no idea. We could only tell them what we did know. Then twenty-five of those soldiers stayed overnight and took off in the big plane the following day."

The missionaries now made the connection with the helicopters and the big plane they had heard. This had occurred soon after they had left Morichal. Surely the guerrilla espionage system had given warning that the army was coming, and the hostages had been hurried out of the village. The trio thanked God that there had been no confrontation between army and guerrillas and no blood shed on their account.

The various captains then called for a meeting with the guerrillas, and, in unison, demanded the release of the missionaries.

The guerrillas asked one of them, Francisco, why he thought the missionaries were so good. Francisco did not hesitate to reply.

"They have done many things for us! They give us medicine when we're sick. They bring us things we need from town in the airplane. They took me to the hospital just last month when I was dying and didn't charge me anything. And *Timoteo* is teaching us the Word of God!"

Tim and Bunny were only told a part of what went on in that meeting. It ended with the guerrillas trying to convince the Indians that nothing would happen to the missionaries.

Meantime, others of the Puinaves were enjoying their freedom to talk with the trio. They looked on as though feasting their eyes on them. In real concern, they asked, "Did they hit you?" "Did they force you to work for them?" "Do they feed you?" "Are you well?"

Tim and Bunny assured them that they were fine and had not been physically mistreated.

Chicho's son, Mario, tried to describe the feelings of the villagers after the trio had been taken to the jungle.

"It was as though one of our children had died. We walked around the village looking for someone to comfort us, but everyone felt the same way. We didn't feel like eating. We would walk by your empty house and feel so sad! Nobody wanted to go fishing. The women didn't feel like working in the garden. So we decided to go visit Francisco downriver and get away from here."

A big lump welled up in Tim's throat, so that he was unable to respond. For them to compare their love for the missionaries with their love for their children was too much for Tim. Tears stung his eyes. He had not realized how much they really cared.

Before the missionaries and Puinaves had to part that day, they made arrangements to keep in touch in the future. In the first place, Tim promised to give a certain message over the radio — a local radio station that many Puinaves listened to — when he got out to safety and all was well.

Then they discussed some future get-together. "Whenever you can come back to us, just let us know," Alberto said, "and we'll move back here. If you cannot come here, then tell us where to go, and we'll make our village there."

Meanwhile, there would be no Morichal for them without the Cains.

Keeping the faith

Missionary escapes captors;

Mission

Continued from Page 1A

a calm, detached manner. It is hard to imagine him in the jungles of South America as he tells the story from inside a home on Military Street in Port Huron. The home belongs to his sister, Kay Squires, and mother, Dorothy

Paul Dye
Was held in jungle

Missionary pilot escapes guerrilla captors

Three others left behind in Columbian jungle,

A missionary pilot has escaped from leftist guerrillas who kidnapped him and three other Americans in Bogota, Colombia, weeks ago. He flew out of the jungle on a foggy moonless night, his lights out, knowing if he had enough ... make it, a spokesman for the missionary group said Friday.

The guerrillas have demanded $130,000 ransom for the three missionaries they still hold, said ... Wyma of the New Tribes Mission of Sanford, Fla.

Paul Dye of Saginaw, Mich., was flying a missionary couple and a copilot out of a remote southeastern village Oct. 5 when they stopped over at Morichal Viejo, 250 miles from the mission headquarters in the central Colombian town of Villavicencio, his

His adventure began Oct. 4 when Tim Cain, a missionary working with the Puinave Indians in southeast Columbia, radioed for a plane. Cain said he was sick and needed help. But in reality, six guerrillas held him and his wife, Bonnie, at gunpoint.

American pilot escapes kidnappers

BOGOTA, Colombia — A missionary pilot has escaped from leftist guerrillas who kidnapped him and three other Americans weeks ago. He flew out of the jungle on a foggy, moonless night, his lights out, not knowing if he had enough fuel to make it, a spokesman for the missionary group said Friday.

The guerrillas have demanded a $130,000 ransom for the three missionaries they still hold, said Mel Wyma of the New Tribes Mission of Sanford, Fla.

Paul Dye, of Saginaw, Mich., was flying a missionary couple and a copilot out of a remote southeastern village on Oct. 5 when they stopped over at Morichal Viejo, 250 miles from the mission headquarters in the central Colombian town of Villavicencio, his wife told the AP. Rebels seized the single-engine plane and flew off with the four Americans, she said.

Dye escaped on Oct. 10, Wyma said in a telephone interview, but did not explain why it wasn't announced earlier.

Newspaper clippings telling of Paul's escape were sent to Mission Headquarters from all around the nation.

After the missionaries and the guerrillas left Morichal, Professor was silent, having observed for the first time the relationship between the Cains and the Puinaves. It was evident he had not seen such love demonstrated before. The next morning, he walked over to the cocoon with the sole purpose of finding out the secret — what made the Indians love these missionaries so much.

"How do you do it?" he asked Tim.

Tim did not try to express it in words.

"Ask *them!*" he answered.

Later that night, Tim tuned in to the Voice of America. He was thoroughly enjoying his little contact with the outside world. Suddenly he heard a reference to the three American missionaries in the hands of the guerrillas, followed by their own names. Then a news note followed that almost bowled the trio over. It said that a ransom note *had* been received by the Mission for $131,000 for the release of Bunny Cain who was "in delicate health."

What a development — after all the promises and clear understanding that they were to be turned over to the Peace Commission! The trio had no way of knowing that the media had only then received the news about the ransom note written October 9, before the knowledge of Paul's escape. Much had gone on in the guerrilla hierarchy since then.

Bunny's hopes of seeing her girls and other loved ones were dashed to the ground. "Lord, what happened?" It seemed her bubble had burst. She turned her head and sobbed silently, not wanting the men to hear her.

Tim had been entertaining real hope, also, but now felt he was seeing the other side of the coin. So these guerrillas had just been lying to them, keeping up their hopes so they would not try to escape! "We will probably not make it out of here alive," Tim concluded, as his first reaction.

Although Bunny hit bottom, she did not stay there. She was reminded quickly that God was still in complete control and that He would be faithful to her *whichever way* it would turn out. As they prayed alone, then together that night, they reaffirmed their trust in God for Him to do what was for their good.

They added, "Lord, keep us resting in You. And won't You please keep things under Your control. Help our families to cope with this news...."

13

To God Be the Glory

Soon after Paul's air drop of letters to the guerrillas, the Mission leaders felt it would be wise to take copies of that message to Bogotá. They wanted to put it personally into the hands of each of the twelve men on the Peace Commission who handled affairs between government and terrorists. Surely these men might help to persuade the F.A.R.C. to release Steve, Tim, and Bunny.

The accomplishing of this goal was much more difficult than the missionary executives had anticipated. They did not know where to turn nor what to do, and any real plan they might tackle seemed blurry. Sometimes, they just sat in offices and waited in vain. In one office, they were waiting for a return phone call. They sat and sat. After the morning and half the afternoon had passed, Macon dared to call back. The man at the other end was waiting for a return call from someone else before he could call back!

So it went, from one place to another. One man, who seemed to be a key man to help them, was out of the country, another on vacation. One man gave advice contrary to counsel that had just been given. So they found themselves waiting on God just a step at a time.

Finally, the air of confusion seemed to clear. They had watched some who were once cooperative begin to drag their feet. So on advice that all felt was right, they saw that it was now time to give the news out to the public. That in itself would keep the situation of the captives before the guerrillas' high command and, hopefully, help. Until that time, God had not given the Mission men any freedom to air the news.

As soon as the Colombia media did their publicizing, there were those who urged the F.A.R.C. to release the prisoners. Even the head of the communist political party did so on television. But there was no immediate sign that the three captives would be set free.

Duane and Mel returned to the United States. Mel took charge of getting the news out to the media from the Sanford Headquarters. He encouraged folks to write their senators. Many did, while others telephoned. Many of these responded immediately and contacted the State Department, who in turn urged the American Embassy to keep the information before the appropriate Colombian authorities. It was important not to let the matter rest. Every little bit helped.

As the story spread in the United States, more of God's people joined in prayer. Hundreds, perhaps thousands who knew nothing of New Tribes Mission, much less the missionaries involved, took on a special burden to keep praying for the three hostages at all hours. Some 1,500 people at the Moody Bible Institute missionary conference prefaced many of their sessions with prayer for the safety of the three missionaries. Continual coverage was given in WMBI newscasting as well as interviews from New Tribes Mission Headquarters over Prime Time America. This, along with mass coverage by other TV stations, newspapers, and radio stations awakened Christians nationwide to the urgent need for prayer.

The Mission men remaining in Colombia had to continue the pursuit of members of the Peace Commission. These gentlemen were responsible to see that the F.A.R.C. held to their peace treaty. It would have been easy by now to give up on *them* and to just say "The battle is the Lord's!" But God urged them to keep "pushing on doors," to leave no stone unturned to find the men of influence who could put pressure on the guerrillas to release the trio. There were rebuffs, but there were "little miracles" too.

One potential friend seemed predisposed to keep from getting involved. As he stood aloof from the waiting missionaries, the phone rang in his office. When he turned back from answering it, his whole attitude had changed.

"That was a friend of mine and a friend of yours," he said, seating himself with them. "He wants me to do anything I can to help you. Now, what would you like me to do?" and the man used his influence from then on to try to get through to the guerrillas that they had made a mistake!

Duane looks back on those days in Colombia with a new insight into how God leads His children. They had asked Him to lead, and at times it would have been easy to wonder if He was still leading them. Duane says, "In the midst of the battle and the confusion, God *does* give guidance and direction if we take the time to wait on Him and walk by faith, and trust that He *is* leading and guiding."

Duane referred in part to the confusion that reigned during the writing of that letter to the F.A.R.C.; yet he was amazed at how well it turned out when he read it over some time later. God had indeed guided the writing of it. Then, too, the waiting in offices all seemed to be battle and confusion, but God was guiding them in that also, as though holding them there until it was the right time for them to get His further instructions.

Out in the jungle, Steve, Tim, and Bunny did not know what was happening to them. They heard on the news that they were to be released to the Peace Commission, yet they dared not get their hopes up too high. God was in control, they were still sure, and their peace in Him remained firm, "whether by life or by death."

Three nights after the confirming of the news that a ransom had been requested for Bunny, Tim was lying awake in the cocoon. Though his position did not permit the tossing and turning he would normally have done, he toyed a bit with the radio. Suddenly, a reporter on Voice of America startled him into full attention:

> "Tonight we have an interview with Mel Wyma of New Tribes Mission about the missionaries who were taken hostage in Colombia.
>
> "Mr. Wyma, where are the immediate families of the hostages?"
>
> Mel's voice rang out clearly, "We have had the Estelle family and the Cain's two girls brought back here to the United States."
>
> "Was there a ransom asked for?"
>
> "Yes, there was; but we cannot pay it."
>
> "Is it true that one of the pilots escaped with the airplane?"
>
> "Yes, it's true. Both he and the plane are safe."
>
> "What is the Mission doing to get the others out of there?"
>
> "Well, we're working with the Peace Commission in Colombia, and it looks hopeful."

All three in the mosquito net had become thoroughly alert. To hear Mel's voice and his outlook was decidedly encouraging. His answer concerning the ransom note only confirmed what they already knew. But that news about their families was a big load off their minds. They felt sure all were being well taken care of; yet, just to *know* where their children were was most satisfying. Bunny felt that for the reporter to ask that particular question was another of God's "little miracles" on their behalf.

On the last day of October, Steve, Tim, and Bunny were taken back to Morichal. There they were to wait for a plane coming for them. The guerrillas were to go with them, so they were left in suspense as to what it was all about. At least, it was more pleasant to stay in the Cains' house than in their crowded "cocoon" in the jungle. Further, Alberto and others were still around and visited them often, assuring Tim that God would soon set them free.

One night passed. No plane.

Another night passed. No plane.

After six nights in the village, the three were ordered back to the jungle to sleep in a guerrilla camp close to the airstrip. That night, they missed the "cocoon!" They were given the Cains' hammocks but without mosquito nets. Bunny could not sleep a wink for the mosquitoes, and the men fared little better.

The following morning, Professor called on the radio to see if a plane was on its way. The voice at the other end sounded hostile.

"When the plane is going to come, I'll let you know!" it bellowed.

The camp cook fixed an early lunch and fed the group at 11 o'clock. At 11:30, a plane flew over just as someone called in over the radio, "Isn't that plane there yet?"

The plane had come for them.

The guerrillas hurried their captives to grab what they could. Quickly, they stuffed things into their two suitcases, and the guards almost ran them to the airstrip. There was no time then to realize that the Cains' more valuable things were at the house while they lugged around their bedding and a change of clothes! At the bottom of an incline on that "roller-coaster strip," they were stopped. The guards used two of Tim's T-shirts to blindfold the men and handed Bunny a red bandana to tie around her eyes. From there they were led to a small twin-engined plane at the other end of the runway. No explanation was made for the blindfolds, but it became evident they were not to see either the plane or the pilot. They did not even know if Professor got on board.

As yet, there was no sense of freedom since the guerrillas were down on the floor with them in that cargo plane, on a sort of platform. If the three leaned back, a gun would jab inescapably into their backs. They flew for two hours and seemed to take a long time in landing. Then two guerrillas led the captives by the hand down into some very tall bushes, well out of sight of the plane. Only then could they remove the blindfolds. The guerrillas hurried them down the bank to the river where they waited some time for a speedboat. When it arrived, there was more waiting while the motorist (the guerrilla who ran the boat) went up the hill. Finally, all was ready, and six people crowded into that small speedboat: the motorist, two guards, and the trio.

Once they pushed off from the shore, they tried to start the motor. Not a sound. The boat merely drifted downriver. A guard called out to shore for help. Help came, but they could not start the motor. Back they went by trail to the airstrip. This time, the three were allowed to walk down the airstrip without being blindfolded since the plane had taken off quickly after landing. But before they got to the end of the runway, they were stopped.

"There's something ahead you can't see," said the guards, and they blindfolded them again.

Little did the missionaries realize that they were on the very airstrip from which Paul had made his escape. Blindfolded, they were skirting around the little circle where the Cessna had been hidden. Steve's guide was not too careful with his blinded ward, and Steve bumped into bushes and trees on the little path leading to the camp. The other guerrilla, with Bunny's hand on one side and Tim's on the other, was more careful. Part way down the path, they took off the blindfolds and allowed them to walk into camp "with their own eyes."

Only then were the missionaries told that Paul had been held in that camp.

"This is where Capitán Pablo slept," they said to Steve, showing him Paul's bed of boards on barrels — still arranged, mattress and all. It was to be Steve's for the night. He made no connection at the time, but it later occurred to him that one of the guards was carrying Paul's leather case wherever he went.

One guerrilla led the Cains straight to his own shelter, took his things elsewhere, and turned his bed over to Tim and Bunny. Narrow as it was, it was still more spacious and airy than the "cocoon."

Early the next morning the three were escorted to the river. There was Professor whom they had last seen in Morichal. With him, one guard, and the motorist, they took off in a speedboat from the port of the campsite. For the next six hours they traveled down the river, turning eventually into a creek where overhanging branches gave relief from the sun. They stopped at a small farm where there was a house and a store that sold pop, beer, crackers, and Vienna sausage. The guerrillas seemed well-acquainted with the place.

"We're going to stop here and have a drink," the guards told them, as they all carefully stepped out of the little boat.

The drink was most welcome, and the captives were fed two little cans of Vienna sausage.

For about an hour, Steve, Tim, and Bunny sat around with the guerrillas, wondering what was going on. Then a speedboat came roaring up with the news that the Peace Commission was indeed coming. The response to this news was surprising. The guerrillas, who had left their big guns behind and only carried pistols on the boat ride, now scurried for places to hide their pistols. There were some present who were carrying cocaine to this spot. They found places to hide it also.

Only now, with the assurance that the Peace Commission representatives were on the way, did Professor announce to the missionary trio why they were there — that they were to be given over into the hands of the Peace Commission to be set free to go back to their families.

Steve, Tim, and Bunny were not certain whether they should "put stock" in this until they could see the Peace Commission themselves. Days had turned into weeks since they had been told this was to happen. Still, they were *moving,* at least, and their hopes rose higher.

Within an hour, a motorboat arrived from upriver. This was a huge *bongo* that was almost too large for the creek. There were three members of the Peace Commission and four members of a Sub-Commission — the latter being three men from the nearest big town and a reporter for a communist paper.

Handshakes were the order of the day. Then the visitors went right to the point. "Where is the old lady? Where is the sick lady?" they asked, looking around.

To the guerrillas and to the Peace Commission, Bunny looked neither old nor sick. In fact, she *felt* no lack of the vegetables and fruit she should have had for her hypoglycemia diet — a fact she attributed to answered prayer. (If only she knew how many people *did* pray for her once the news came out that she was "in poor health." People added a prayer for her health to the prayer for Tim's.)

But what made the outside world think she was old? It turned out that the last digits of their years of birth, '50 and '52, had been written, following their interrogation, as Tim's and Bunny's actual ages.

The six men of the Commission sat around a large table which did duty as a "conference table." They were looking at Steve, Tim, and Bunny.

"You folks are sitting around this table looking so calm and at peace, while we're the ones who are all nervous and uptight about this whole situation!"

So began the release to the Peace Commission.

First on the agenda was to have a picture taken of the missionaries together with the Peace Commission members. This, on their part, would be important for the media. Then there were further formalities. There was a speech by the Peace Commission representative to the guerrillas. Now it was Professor's turn to make a formal declaration on the part of the guerrillas.

"As a member of the high command of the F.A.R.C., I have made an investigation of these three North Americans. I find that the accusation that they were members of the CIA is not true.

"On the contrary, these people are a benefit to the Indian society. They are doing a good job in the jungle, and they are invited by us to return there." The missionaries all but dropped their mouths open in surprise at this one!

And that concluded the ceremony.

The women who lived on the farm then brought in some tender beef they had prepared for the company and served it along with french fries to everyone. The reporter took his turn and had each of the missionaries speak into his tape recorder.

"How do you feel?" he specifically asked Bunny. He had taken pictures of her several times during the meal, always just as she opened her mouth.

"Were you treated well?"

"Did anyone ask you for ransom money?" This one was strange, and, of course, the answer was negative since the money was requested of the Mission, not of the trio.

The missionaries gave on-the-spot answers: Yes, Bunny felt fine. Yes, they were treated well (toward the last). No one had asked *them* for ransom money. Predictably, their replies were exploited as proof of the fact that they had been merely *detained* and had not been *kidnapped*. There had been no chance to tell or even think of how they had been cut off from all communication with loved ones, had had their home and belongings confiscated, had been harassed as spies, and had been illegally ejected from the work to which they were giving their lives.

Officially now, the three were no longer hostages, having been turned over to the Peace Commission to get them back to Bogotá safely.

The parting from Professor was a firm handshake. Tim was surprised to find a caring look there. In fact, Professor's eyes were moist. Tim discovered he *did* have a heart.

Things looked very hopeful to the trio for full freedom. But they were not yet on the plane for Bogotá. In fact, they were sure they would be stopping in a town or two where guerrillas and cocaine-growers were free to roam.

The missionaries and the three members of the Peace Commission then traveled to the town of Calamar in the huge *bongo*. It was 6 p.m. when they arrived at the town. The whole group was fed royally in a restaurant. Then the Peace Commission reported to Bogotá by radio that the three missionaries were officially free.

Steve, Tim, and Bunny pinched themselves to see if it were really true. It had been thirty-three days since the guerrillas kidnapped the Cains in their own home and thirty-two days since Steve and the plane had been captured. Soon they would be seeing their loved ones again. How utterly faithful God had been to them!

That night, they were escorted by three Peace Commission representatives — minus guerrillas, guns, or hand grenades — to the house of a young Colombian Roman Catholic priest.

"Here," said the leader, "we're going to put you religious people together." As he left the trio at the door, his parting words were, "Have a good ecumenical evening!" With that the Peace Commission representatives took off to sleep in the local hospital.

The missionaries were given two beds in one room while other people slept in hammocks strung in the priest's front room.

Apparently the priest was accustomed to turning his house into a lodging place for strangers.

Just after Tim and Bunny had fallen asleep, there was a light knock at the door. Steve, near the open bedroom door not far from the hallway, saw the priest open the door and admit a young man to a hammock in the hallway. Steve felt instinctively that this man was a guerrilla, judging from his furtive glances around.

Don't tell me they're not through with us yet, he said to himself, and that we're not really free after all! Steve could not settle down to sleep for a while.

Suddenly there was a loud knock at the front door. A voice called from outside, "It's the police." Immediately the man in the hammock scooted out the back way, never to return that night.

"Are the American hostages here?" one of the policemen asked loudly.

"Sí, señor," the priest answered, without going to the door. "They're here, but they're sleeping."

"Just checking," said the policeman.

It was through the police office that word arrived at Villavicencio and from there to the missionaries who were waiting in Bogotá. At 11:30 that night, Macon answered the phone in the Mission guest home.

"Your people are free! They will be in Bogotá tomorrow!"

Rumors had come so often those past few days, in the press and over the radio, but this time they had it from a reliable source. God had done the impossible in answer to believing prayer. Soon everyone in the guest home was awake and up to join in the rejoicing. Much praise went up to God. Calls went home to be relayed that night or the next morning all across the country.

The following morning, the three flew in one small plane and the Peace Commission in another to San José. The very name San José was rather horrifying to Tim. It was notorious for traffic in cocaine and for guerrillas. But there they waited some six-and-a-half hours until arrangements were made for commercial airlines to pick them up and take them to Bogotá.

At the Mission apartment in Bogotá, the Dyes, Macon Hare, Connie Cain, and others excitedly awaited the arrival of the three. The day seemed to drag on. But surely it was not a false report. Four times Pat Dye had prepared a special meal for them. Yellow ribbons were tied expectantly inside the house. Macon and others, excluding Paul, were meeting every plane from the San José direction.

Finally that afternoon, November 7, Macon's car drove up to the apartment with all three of the one-time hostages. Bunny jumped out as perky as ever. Tim was looking good in spite of having lost some weight. Steve looked just as great to Paul as the day they parted, in spite of the fact that he had worn the same jeans day and night for those thirty-three days! Health-wise, they never felt better!

One and all in the Mission apartment marveled at the mercy of God in freeing the three, as He had Paul, for further service. Questions and answers between Paul and the other three tumbled back and forth around the table and into the night. There was one great similarity in their experiences: that God had had to deal with their hearts first before they truly rested in Him and left Him free to work.

Each one was anxious to share the Scriptures God had made so special to them at different stages of their captivity. Steve said, "The Psalms are so good, and Genesis and Revelation — and everything in between!" Then he summed up his impression of the whole ordeal.

"I would not wish it on anyone else, but I wouldn't trade the experience for anything. I learned so many spiritual lessons. I can honestly say it was a privilege."

By the time the missionaries realized how many around the world had been praying for them, they saw more than ever that there was no way they could feel it was just *their* prayer God had answered. Not only was prayer going up for them from the Puinaves, but from tribal groups with other missions besides New Tribes in Colombia, Brazil, Venezuela, Bolivia, Philippines, and many others. They soon began to receive letters from around the world to this effect.

One missionary to the Ayorés* in Paraguay wrote:

> "One of the biggest blessings I have enjoyed seeing is the way that the Ayoré Indians' hearts have been touched deeply by happenings outside of their own little world. During the Colombian crisis, the Ayorés were fervently praying, constantly asking for information, being deeply involved in the struggle. When I told Mateo of the release of the missionaries, I was almost overwhelmed when I saw tears starting to fill his eyes.
>
> "When we tell the Indians of special prayer requests, they regularly remember them and pray, expecting God to work!"

* This is the same tribe that killed Paul's father and four others in 1943.

The four hostages reunited in the Bogotá guest house

Back in the United States, there were people unknown to the missionaries who prayed, often losing sleep to pray. These were individuals, intercessory groups and those who carried on prayer chains. Several churches of the Cherokee Indians who worked with the Mission's linguists-in-training kept up faithful petitions to God for the hostages.

The Dyes, Cains, and Steve traveled together to Florida for a meeting with the Executive Committee, Betsy Estelle joining them there. Though they were hurried through Miami, not so at their destination in Orlando, closest airport to Mission Headquarters. There were welcome placards in the terminal and a big sign "TO GOD BE THE GLORY" that the Mission had been allowed to put up. That part was just as the four would have had it.

However, the first to work their way through the crowd were the reporters and the TV cameras. Tim especially was dismayed by the "show." He was much like Peter after the healing of the lame man,

> *"...why look ye so earnestly on us, as though by our own power or holiness we had made this man to walk?"* (Acts 3:12)

Tim said, "It was as though we were getting the glory when everything was focused on us. But it was God! We were just tools that God used. It's God's story, not ours! Even the guerrillas...God used them to work in our lives. He just had them wrapped around His little finger!"

All were convinced, too, that God not only worked miracles for them to be freed from the guerrillas but had worked out an intricate plan for each of the captives, to carry out His own purposes. It became apparent that He had even *put* them in the position they were in, in order to show Himself strong on their behalf.

On the day immediately following Paul's escape, he had had to clear the red tape connected with his landing the Cessna in a field. He found himself having to answer questions by some who had a legal right to interrogate him. In that group were two generals of the Colombian army who had just heard of his escape. Rather than answer every question, Paul asked if he might tell his whole story. He wanted to get across that it was *God* who got him out and not his own ingenuity.

He told it in detail, Scripture and all, letting them see the power of God's Word in his life as a believer.

When he finished the story, everyone was silent, spellbound. Then a general broke the silence, "That was better than the movies!" With that he came over to Paul and voiced his deep impression.

"Paul, if you were my man, I would give you one of my highest honors! But you're not my man. You're God's!

"I see three things here: First, as far as we know you are the only man to have ever escaped from the F.A.R.C. Second, you took off at night in the dark and in heavy ground fog. And third, you landed at night in the dark without a scratch. Now that has to be God!"

Paul inwardly worshipped the One who was getting the credit. "Thank You, Lord!"

The second general gave clear assent to all that the first had said. Then he walked with Paul out to where a missionary who had not yet heard Paul's story was waiting. As the general left Paul with the missionary, he said pointedly, "Paul is a brave man; but that's not what saved him. And he's an intelligent man — key in his shoe and all that — but that's not what saved him. It was his faith that saved him."

The missionary agreed that it had to be God who enabled Paul to escape, though he did not know yet how it was brought about. He looked a bit blank so the general drove the point home as he had seen it.

The four much-prayed-for captives disembark in Florida. (Cains not visible)

"Do you know what he *did?*" He summed it up with emphasis: "He took the Word of God. He applied it to his life. And *it worked!*"

Another "Thank You, Lord" went up in silence from Paul's heart. To think that these great men in the world could see what he saw...that God's Word is just as powerful and wonderful today as when it was written!

Next had followed the voluntary surrender of Steve, Tim, and Bunny by the terrorists — a miracle act of God. And no doubt it was another *first* for those guerrillas.

As Paul told his story to the church back home, God's people realized the magnitude of the miracle which had brought about his escape and the trio's release. They were thrilled that the "Lord God of Elijah" still lives today. Then Paul reminded them of something else.

"If the outcome of our situation had *not* turned out as it did...if all four of us had been killed, God would still be God. He would still be holy, just, and righteous. He would still be the same loving and caring God that He is."

But God was pleased to work things out just as He did for his own purposes — for His children to sit up and take notice.

To the world, then, and to Christians everywhere today, God seems to be saying, in words like those so aptly expressed by the general:

"Just take My Word and apply it to your life! I'm the same powerful God to work for *you* as I ever was with My people of old."